One City – Many Communities

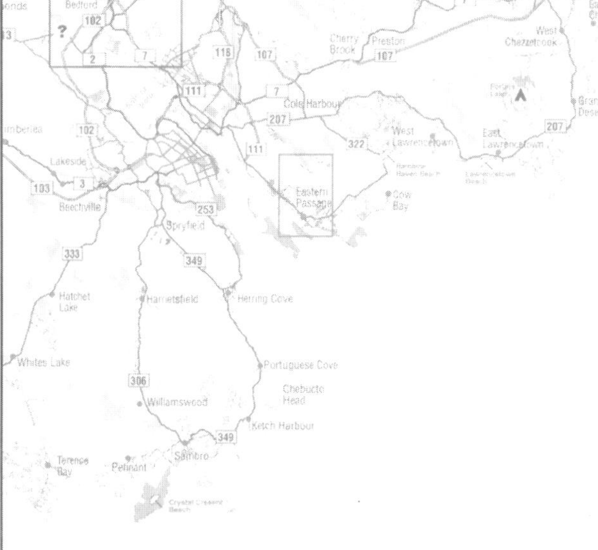

This book is dedicated to the descendants of those families who settled in the Halifax Regional Municipality, 1749 to 1999.

Nimbus Publishing Limited
PO Box 9301, Station A, Halifax, NS B3K 5N5
(902)455-4286

Cover photo credits: Centre photo—Russ Heinl. Clockwise, top right—1. Doug Leahy; 2. – 8. P. M. Franklin; 9. Steve Farmer; 10. Wally Hayes; 11. Halifax Tourism, Culture & Heritage; 12. P. M. Franklin.

Design:Arthur Carter
Printed and bound in Canada

Canadian Cataloguing in Publication Data
Withrow, Alfreda
One City, Many Communities
ISBN 1-55109-294-8
1. Halifax (N.S.: Regional Municipality) — History, Local. I. Title
FC2346.4.W57 1999 971.6'225 C99-950209-3
F1039.5.H17W57 1999

Key to Image Captions:
AW: Alfreda Withrow
HRM: Halifax Regional Municipality
NSARM: Nova Scotia Archives and Record Management
MRM: Musquodoboit Railway Museum
MSHS: Mainland South Historical Society

Nimbus Publishing acknowledges the financial support of the Government of Canada through the Book Publishing Industry Development Program (BPIDP), and through Canada Council for our publishing activities.

Contents

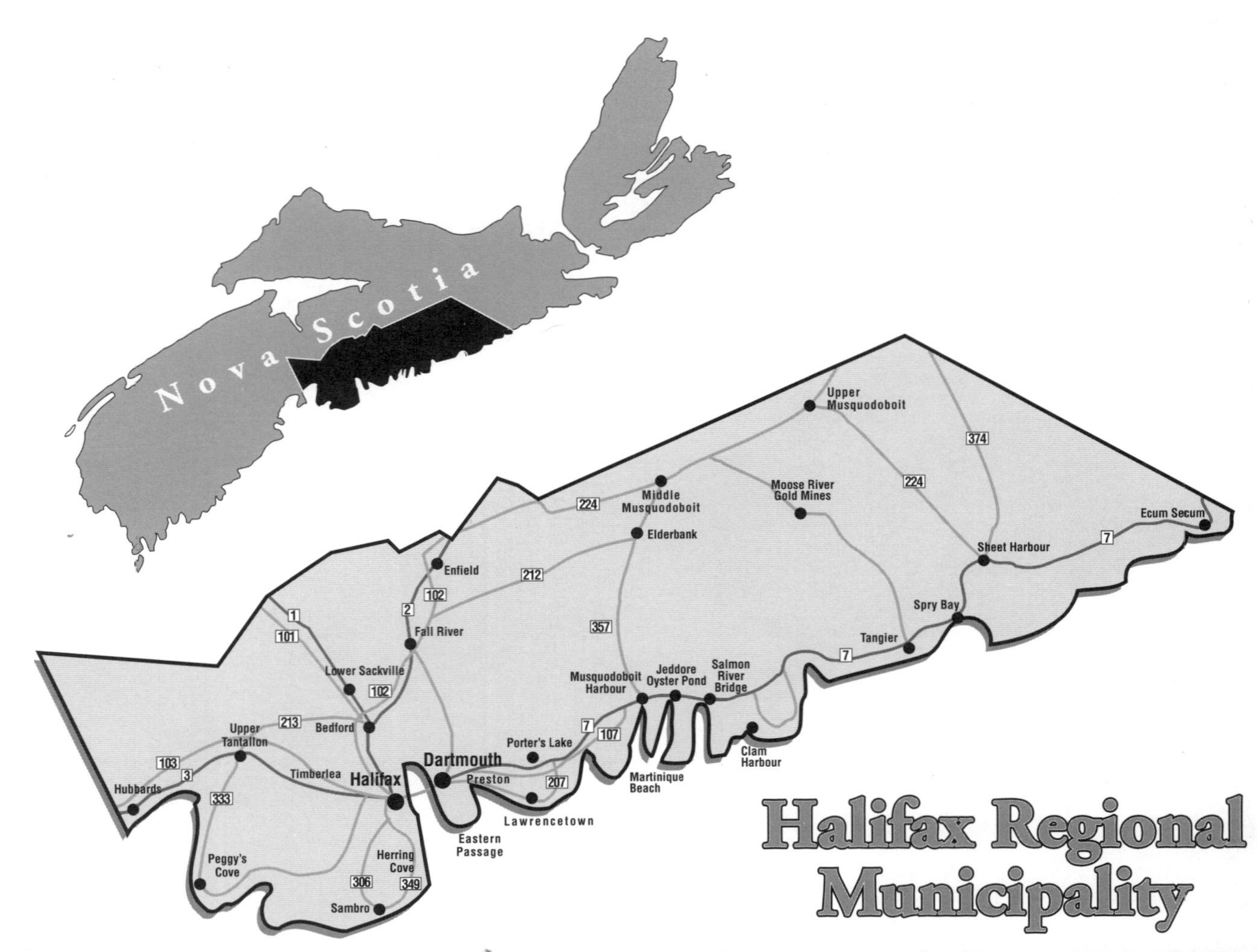

Halifax Regional Municipality

Preface

From January 1, 1999 to December 31, 2000, the Halifax Regional Municipality (HRM) is celebrating both the Millennium and the 250th anniversary of European settlement in this region. This book, *One City—Many Communities*, was undertaken to discover the unique histories of the more than two hundred communities that form the newly amalgamated region. It is designed to give citizens and visitors alike an insight into the commonalities that give us a shared sense of place as we go forward into the next millennium.

When we first began this book there were concerns about the possible loss of community identity that might have come about through the amalgamation of Halifax, Dartmouth, Bedford, and the County of Halifax. In order to discover community identity we decided to present three or four aspects that have helped to define each settlement as a unique place today. This is not intended to be a complete history of each community. But it will give readers an insight into the people, cultures and industries that have shaped the nearly 200 communities that citizens now call "home." For example, we have tried to determine which cultures contributed to the settlement of each community, which family names are associated with pioneer settlements, what industries first developed and which particular people, stories and events have shaped a community's life.

The information contained here will prove particularly useful to long time residents seeking to recall family names associated with settlements, new residents seeking to find out more about a community they have moved into, students tracing historical trends and visitors travelling through HRM who are interested in its people, places, and events.

The photographs that accompany each community history are a combination of archival collections and, where these were not available, present day images.

Our work has shown us that the communities that make up the Halifax Regional Municipality are a reflection of the diversity and history of Nova Scotia. By discovering the common themes that have shaped the region we may begin to feel more a part of the larger community.

This book is organized into ten chapters, each chapter being one of the ten cultural tourism areas being developed within HRM. The areas are grouped according to geographic proximity, cultural similarity and family surname commonalities. It is the expectation of HRM that these areas will provide a basis for regional marketing, promotion and development initiatives. Time will tell.

Mayor Walter Fitzgerald,
Halifax Regional Municipality

As Chair of the Halifax Regional Municipality 2000 Millennium Committee, I am proud to be associated with the publication of *One City—Many Communities*, a wonderful collection of unique stories from the nearly 200 communities that make up the Halifax Regional Municipality.

Students, educators, citizens, and visitors alike will find this book an invaluable tool in learning about the diverse backgrounds, cultures, and histories that are such a vital part of our region. This book makes an important contribution to the cultural evolution of the Municipality by recognizing those citizens who helped develop our individual communities.

As we mark the 250th anniversaries of Halifax and Dartmouth and the arrival of the new millennium, we at the Millennium Committee are dedicated to incorporating all communities and residents into the many exciting celebrations planned 1999 and 2000.

On behalf of the Millennium Committee, I would like to sincerely thank all those responsible for *One City—Many Communities*: author, Alfreda Withrow; the editorial and production departments at Nimbus Publishing; and the many staff members of the Halifax Regional Municipality, particularly the Tourism, Culture, and Heritage Department.

One City—Many Communities will become a legacy to treasure for all of us who live and work within the Halifax Regional Municipality. I hope you will enjoy reading it as much as I did.

Jack Keith, Chair of the Halifax Regional Municipality
2000 Millennium Committee

The Millennium Committee is proud to present *One City—Many Communities*; many thanks to the HRM2000 corporate sponsors for their generous support of the project.

Introduction

For centuries, the Mi'kmaq camped on the shores of Halifax Harbour. Evidence of their camps can be found as far west as Terence Bay, as far east as Liscomb, around the edges of Halifax Harbour and on MacNab's Island. The Mi'kmaq were a nomadic people, camping by the shore in warm months to fish and following caribou and moose herds inland to the Musquodoboit Valley during winter. They left behind some evidence of their passage such as artifacts and arrowheads, and a few well worn trails.

Acadians also lived in what is today the Halifax Regional Municipality, particularly in the Chezzetcook area. In 1755 when Governor Charles Lawrence ordered the expulsion of all Acadians who would not sign an oath of allegiance to the King of Great Britain, many of the Chezzetcook Acadians fled to the woods to hide. Most of them were captured and instead of being expelled were imprisoned in Halifax until amnesty was granted. After their release, they returned to find their farmlands taken over by settlers from New England.

A Notman portrait photograph of Mi'kmaq women taken ca. 1880. (NSARM)

French names such as Dauphinee or Jollimore can be found scattered around the region, particularly in the St. Margaret's Bay area. In the early 1600s, Samuel de Champlain sailed into the bay and mapped it. On one map he shows it as Baie St. Marguerite. And a burial ground found on the shores of the Bedford Basin which was thought to be either the graves of Mi'kmaqs or shipwrecked French sailors, turned out to be Acadians who had lived in a nearby community.

Permanent settlement of the region followed the founding of Halifax in 1749. The garrison at Halifax was established to protect English settlers from attack by the French and their Mi'kmaq allies and to establish an armed presence to counter a perceived threat from the French fortress at Louisbourg on Cape Breton Island.

Governor Edward Cornwallis, founder of Halifax, was a good strategist. He organized the founding of Dartmouth within a year and soon had a ferry service running between the two towns. He arranged for Protestant families from the Rhine region of Germany and from Protestant areas of France to settle in the Lunenburg area. His intention was to counter the influence of the Catholic Acadian settlements along the area. He immediately started road construction along the Mi'kmaq foot paths around the Bedford Basin and through dense woods to the Minas Basin on the Bay of Fundy. And to protect the road, he ordered John Gorham's rangers to build Fort Sackville at the head of the Bedford Basin. Cornwallis encouraged settlement in the Halifax/Dartmouth area and made land available to pioneers who were willing to establish permanent homesteads along the Eastern Shore of Nova Scotia.

Cornwallis created the conditions that made permanent settlement possible. Settlement took place largely in four waves. First to arrive in 1750 were the Foreign Protestants from France and Germany. In the 1760s, Planters arrived from the New England States. The Loyalists moved to Nova Scotia around 1783-84, many settling in the Halifax region. These were mostly settlers from the New England states who had sided with the British during the American Revolution. The last group followed on the heels of the War of 1812-14.

What is remarkable, particularly in the rural areas of Halifax Regional Municipality, is the number of descendants of the original families who still live in the areas where their ancestors first received land grants. The grant system, which went on for more than 100 years, gave land to settlers who promised to abide by certain conditions, primarily that they would clear a portion of their land within a specified time period. Many of the earliest grants, those issued just after the founding of Halifax, were offered to disbanded soldiers, usually officers, or families of distinction. Many of these people had no intention of living on their lands. They saw them as investments and would then recruit immigrants to settle on their grants. But there were others—Foreign Protestants, Planters, and Loyalists—who lived on their lands, built homesteads, and farmed or fished.

In August 1759, ten years after the town of Halifax was settled, the boundaries of Halifax County were drawn up. Originally the boundary lines encompassed a large geographical area of Nova Scotia. These boundaries were frequently redrawn until 1880 when they were finally defined to those of today. On April 1, 1996 the cities of Halifax and Dartmouth, the town of Bedford and the existing communities within Halifax County were amalgamated into one region now known as the Halifax Regional Municipality.

Chapter One

HALIFAX/ DARTMOUTH

- Halifax
- Armdale
- Dutch Village
- Fairview
- Africville
- Halifax Harbour Islands:
  George's Island
  MacNab's Island
  Devil's Island
  Lawlor's Island
- Dartmouth
- Eastern Passage, Shearwater
- Cow Bay
- Cole Harbour

Above photo:
A photograph of R. Short's engraving depicting how St. Paul's Anglican Church looked in 1775. (NSARM)

INTRODUCTION

Each of the nearly two hundred individual communities that make up Halifax Regional Municipality, evolved slowly after Halifax was settled in 1749. Once the town had been divided into small building lots, settlers began to build a palisade around the boundaries of the military outpost as protection against possible attack by Mi'kmaq or French raids.

The Mi'kmaq regularly camped on the shores of Halifax Harbour and the Bedford Basin. There is some evidence that small Acadian settlements dotted the basin as well. Certainly the Mi'kmaq were still hunting and fishing in the area and in several surrounding communities such as St. Margaret's Bay, MacNab's Island and Dartmouth, when the British arrived in 1749. The Acadians and Mi'kmaq had lived in harmony with each other for over 150 years, but all that was to change with the arrival of the British garrison at Halifax. Within six years, the Acadians had been expelled. Those who fled to the woods and were captured spent several years as prisoners in Halifax until a general amnesty was declared. And of those who were deported and then returned, most found their homes burned and their lands settled by English-speaking colonists, many of whom were New England Planters.

A Mi'kmaq encampment situated on the outskirts of the town of Dartmouth ca. 1900. (NSARM)

HALIFAX

In June of 1749, the *Sphinx*, with Colonel Edward Cornwallis on board, sailed into Halifax Harbour. Accompanying him were 2,545 Europeans, consisting of soldiers, sailors, tradesmen, and their families. The site had been chosen by Cornwallis for its natural harbour overlooked by an imposing hill. Here, he realized he could build a garrison to protect the town from attack. Cornwallis named the town Halifax in honour of George Montagu Dunk, second Earl of Halifax, President of the London Board of Trade in 1749, and Cornwallis's sponsor.

Cornwallis's settlers included hardened soldiers who had fought in the Austrian War and knew well the hardships involved in carving settlements out of wilderness; a few doctors, midwives, schoolmasters, clergymen, and tradesmen. A number of Foreign Protestants, most of German or French origin who were fleeing religious persecution in their own lands along the upper Rhine River arrived a few years later.

Many Foreign Protestants and their families were given farmland in and around the town of Lunenburg and had, by 1753, moved down the South Shore. Within thirty years many second and third generation Foreign Protestants had left family farms along the South Shore for the Eastern Shore where they farmed, fished, and began lumbering and sawmill enterprises.

A photograph of an engraving (ca. 1770) showing fortifications in Point Pleasant Park. (NSARM)

Within a few years of the founding of Halifax, a civil government had been established. It included the governor and a council of six chosen from among the settlers. The names of some of the settlers are familiar to Halifax residents who live or work along Inglis, Salter, Blowers, Almon, Robie, Young, or Smith streets. An election for council members held in 1758 was a milestone in the development of democratically elected governments in North America.

Much of the military construction in and around Halifax took place while Prince Edward, Duke of Kent, was stationed here from 1796 to 1800. He was responsible for renovations made to the fort at Citadel Hill, for the construction of the batteries and Martello Tower armories at Point Pleasant Park, as well as for fortification located on some of the islands in the mouth of Halifax Harbour. In fact, by the time Prince Edward returned to England, he had fortified the harbour from York Redoubt to Point Pleasant Park, across the mouth of the harbour to the Dartmouth side. He also left his trademark—a fascination with round architecture on non-military edifices, including the round St. George's Anglican Church on Brunswick Street and the music rotunda along the Bedford Highway. The latter was built for his French mistress, Julie St. Laurent.

Market day taking place near Cheapside and Bedford Row, ca. 1890. (NSARM)

There has always been a military presence in Halifax, particularly naval. Here, ships set out to battle the Americans at sea during both the American Revolution and the War of 1812. Here, convoys gathered during both World Wars to cross the dangerous Atlantic, carrying supplies to war-torn Europe. Today the eastern part of Canada's naval command is stationed in Halifax.

The tiny military outpost founded by Cornwallis soon grew into a flourishing town. By the time Halifax was incorporated as a city in 1841, it had schools, universities, libraries, churches, and a seat for government. (Province House, built in 1819, which houses the provincial legislature was designed by two architects, John Merrick and Richard Scott.) There were coffee shops whose patrons delighted in arguing politics and more newspapers per capita than anywhere else in North America. Politicians such as Joseph Howe, publisher of *The Novascotian*, argued the need for responsible government (politicians elected by the people to work on behalf of the people) and in 1848, Halifax became the seat of the first fully elected legislature in British North America.

Boating on the North West Arm. (NSARM)

The economy continued to expand as the well-educated middle class began to emerge. Those with new-found wealth built expensive homes in what is today Halifax's South End and established parks and gardens for their enjoyment. The Public Gardens with its grand Victorian walkways, flowerbeds, and bandstand, was first planted in 1837. Point Pleasant, once part of the Duke of Kent's defense systems, was given to the people of Halifax for 999 years by a grateful Queen Victoria for an annual rent of one shilling.

Many of those who worked in the new industries lived near their places of work in Halifax's North End. It was this part of the city that was devastated following the Halifax Explosion of December 6, 1917, when two ships collided in Halifax Harbour resulting in a tremendous explosion as one, a munitions ship, blew up.

A view of the North West Arm in 1871 with Robert Morrow's estate "Bircham" situated near the shore. (NSARM)

The west end area was developed following World War Two, when soldiers and sailors returned to take up civilian life in Halifax and needed inexpensive housing for themselves and their families.

Other families began to settle in communities on the outskirts, such as Armdale, Fairview, or Rockingham. That drift towards suburban living has continued throughout the twentieth century as improved roads made travel easier.

Today the city has a population consisting of many different ethnic groups and professions. The city's architecture depicts much of the story of Halifax from the St. Paul's Anglican Church opposite City Hall, built in 1750, to the glass-fronted Purdy's Wharf tower with pillars driven into the sea bottom, built over two hundred years later. St. Paul's is the oldest Protestant church in Canada and the only building still standing from the time of Governor Cornwallis.

ARMDALE

The community of Armdale is located at the head of the North West Arm near the rotary. One of the earliest settlers was John Hosterman, a

German, who arrived in 1786 when the area was known as North West Arm, and established a grist mill on Chocolate Lake—one of the first commercial enterprises in the area. Over the years, the lake became a popular swimming spot in summer and skating rink in winter.

In the 1860s, Sir Charles Tupper, one of the Fathers of Confederation, established his estate near the North West Arm on what today is Armview Avenue, and named it "Armdale." Here, Sir Charles would watch yachts sailing up and down "the Arm."

Cows grazing on the pasture lands near Simpson's Department store during the early 1940s. (NSARM)

Former residence of the Tupper family known as "Armdale" with Charles Jr., Sophie and Frances Tupper standing in the front yard ca. 1885. (NSARM)

Over the years residents built churches, opened private schools and established a number of commercial enterprises. Many of the families who played important roles in the development of Armdale were descendants of some of the settlers that arrived with Governor Cornwallis in 1749. They included families with the names of Piers, Hathaway, Fenerty, Balcom, Billman, Lear, and Manual.

Business development continued throughout the nineteenth century. In the early 1800s, the Melville Nail Manufacturing Company and Iron Foundry was established. By 1880 two entrepreneurs by the names of Henderson and Potts were operating a paint factory. George Murray owned a general store that later became a drug store, and the Ellis family opened another store. John Keddy ran a stone quarry on what today is Quarry Road, just off the St. Margaret's Bay Road. In 1916, residents decided to name their community Armdale after Sir Charles Tupper's family estate.

Photograph taken ca. 1893 of Sir Charles Tupper (1821–1915) with his son, Charles H. Tupper and his grandson, Charles Tupper, Jr. (NSARM)

It is difficult to imagine, but as late as the 1940s, the land near the Armdale Rotary consisted mainly of pastureland. One of the last farms to disappear belonged to the Keatings; it was situated at the top of Keating Road where it joins Crown Drive. Twenty years later, Keating could still be seen driving his horse and buggy around the rotary, causing traffic jams. When Simpsons Department store was built at today's West End Mall, people travelled by tram to Armdale to shop. They found it difficult to believe that anyone would put a department store so far from the main shopping district of downtown Halifax.

In time, private residences began to replace the country cottages that surrounded the North West Arm as land owners divided properties into smaller building lots. The population increased as bus routes extended into rural areas with paved roads making travel by car easier. As with many of the former suburbs that skirted the city of Halifax, Armdale became a part of the city on January 1, 1969.

Dutch Village

Dutch (Deutche) Village was originally a German settlement. Many of the Protestant German immigrants, who came to Nova Scotia in 1749, were granted land in this part of the city that they referred to as "Westermolt" or "Westernwold," meaning "wester (west) forest." Deutche was mistakenly anglicized as "Dutch" by British settlers.

Among the German families who settled in the community were those with the names of Deal, Frederick, Gebhardt, Hiltz, Hirshmann, Meisner, Merkel, Shaffner, Schmidt, Schultz, Westhoefer (Westhaver), and Wentzel. Another resident was Titus Smith, a naturalist and philosopher. His family were Loyalists who arrived during the 1780s. Smith was recognized for his extensive knowledge of botany and natural history, and Titus Avenue at the top end of Dutch Village Road is named in his honour. He was called the "Father of Environmentalists" and the "Dutch Village

The old arm bridge situated at the head of the North West Arm, with the Charles Geizer's blacksmith shop situated on the west side of the bridge ca. 1870. (NSARM)

Looking east on Chebucto Road towards the intersection of the Quinpool and Dutch Village Roads ca. 1920, prior to the Armdale Rotary being constructed. (NSARM)

Philosopher." In 1801 he was appointed by Governor Wentworth to study the plants, rocks, birds, animals, and fish found throughout the province. This study, which began as a fifty-day project, lasted a lifetime.

Andrew Downs was another naturalist who established the first zoological gardens in North America in 1847 at the head of the North West Arm and along Dutch Village Road. He called his home "Walton Cottage"—a cairn stands today where the entrance to his estate once stood.

Fairview

The Fairview community is located southwest of Bedford Basin and approximately five kilometers from downtown Halifax. The area has been called Dutch Village, Geizer Mountain, and even Squirreltown. For a while the area was known as Three Mile House, after a way-station located in the area for travellers to stop and refresh themselves. The name was officially changed to Fairview in 1941, when it was used for the first time on a Federal Census. A nearby cemetery established in 1892 was also renamed Fairview Cemetery.

The cemetery, located on Windsor Street, was the former property of the

The first St. John's Anglican Church was originally located within the cemetery situated off of Kempt Road, not far from where Three Mile House was once located ca. 1890. (NSARM)

A Notman portrait of George Wright (ca. 1885), a prominent Halifax businessman who lost his life during the fateful sinking of the *Titanic* in 1912. (NSARM)

Veith family. Originally thirty acres were purchased and called Greenwood Cemetery. It is here that many of the victims of the *Titanic* are buried. The *Titanic* sank on its maiden voyage in 1912 between the coasts of Newfoundland and Nova Scotia after hitting an iceberg, and the bodies were brought to Nova Scotia for burial. The city took over the maintenance of the cemetery in 1944.

Few residential homes were built in the Fairview area until after World War Two. As with other parts of Halifax it was amalgamated with the city on the first of January 1969.

AFRICVILLE

Africville, predominantly an area once settled by Black families, was a thriving community located in a part of the city that is now called Seaview Park. At first it was referred to as Campbell Road (now Barrington Street). In the 1860s it was known as "The Road." The area was officially named Africville by 1900.

The Seaview Park Memorial was erected in 1988 and dedicated to the first Black settlers and the former residents of the Africville community. 1999 (AW)

Many of those who first settled here were descendants of Black refugees of the War of 1812. The district was first settled in 1848 by William Brown and William Arnold. Slowly other families joined them, with such names as Carvey, Mantley, Howe, Dixon, Byers, Carter, and Flint. A number of residents moved to Africville from the nearby Black communities of Hammonds Plains and Preston in search of steady employment.

Africville was a tight-knit community. Education and religion played an important role in the lives of its inhabitants. The families built and maintained their own school, hired and boarded teachers. The Africville School was closed in 1953, when the children were integrated into the Halifax educational system. The Seaview African United Baptist Church also served a major role in the lives of the residents. Not only was it a place of worship but it also provided a place for various gatherings such as weddings, funerals, or baptisms.

Many of the residents worked as seamen, domestics, truckers, stonemasons, and pullmen on the trains, and supplemented their food by fishing, planting small gardens, or raising chickens and pigs. During the 1950s and 1960s, many of the younger generation left Africville in search of work, moving as far away as the United States. However, other families moved into the community, including the Vembs from Norway and the Steeds from the West Indies. Nevertheless, the population continued to decrease.

During the late 1960s and early 1970s, amid controversy and dissension, Halifax city officials decided to relocate the residents of Africville to other areas of Halifax. Today the spirit of the community is kept alive through the efforts of many former residents who organized the Africville Genealogical Association in 1982. Each summer the association holds a reunion at Seaview Park of former residents and their descendants, giving them an insight into their heritage and culture.

Halifax Harbour Islands

There are four islands situated at the mouth of Halifax Harbour named George's, MacNab's, Devil's, and Lawlor's Islands. After the arrival of the British in 1749, the islands became part of Halifax's defense system, with fortifications built on them. Many families also settled on the islands, most of who were involved in the fishing industry. They built homes and schools for their children and rowed to nearby Eastern Passage to attend church. It was not until the advent of motorized boats, which allowed the fishermen to live on the mainland and still reach rich fishing areas with ease, that the islands were slowly de-populated.

George's Island

George's Island is located in the middle of Halifax Harbour and was named in the early 1700s for King George II of Great Britain. It was once an important part of Halifax's defense systems and, even to this day, stories of executions, hidden tunnels, and buried pirates' treasure are a part of its folklore.

A two-storey wooden building used as the Royal Engineers' married quarters located in Fort Charlotte on St. George's Island in 1877. (NSARM)

In 1750, Governor Cornwallis had the first fort built on the island. It is said to have been named Fort Charlotte in the late 1790s by the Duke of Kent in honour of his mother, Queen Charlotte. For over seventy years, construction of the fortification was continuous. Over the years it changed from a simple earthen battery to a masonry fortification with a Martello-shaped tower in the centre of the fort. By the turn of the twentieth century, George's Island was no longer useful as a military fort. It was used for the storage of submarine mines to destroy U-boats during World Wars One and Two.

A view of Halifax's Harbour with St. George's Island visible from Citadel Hill in 1884. (NSARM)

In 1965, George's Island became a national historic site. Parks

Canada is responsible for its preservation and has been restoring Fort Charlotte. Hopefully, the island and its fortifications will one day be open to the public.

MacNab's Island

MacNab's Island, situated at the mouth of the harbour, has benefited both the French and the English who at one time or another had control of this part of Nova Scotia.

There is evidence that the French first surveyed MacNab's as early as 1711, building rudimentary fortifications on the island and naming it "Ils de Chibouquetou." Within twenty-one years, it was known as Scarborough Island, then Cornwallis Island in honour of Edward Cornwallis after the founding of Halifax in 1749.

The Royal Engineers conducted field service work on McNab's Island ca. 1900. (NSARM)

The Mi'kmaq used the island as a summer camp until approximately 1760, although the land had been given to Governor Cornwallis's brothers as part of a land grant in 1752. The Cornwallis brothers never lived there, however, and in 1783, Peter McNab purchased the island from the Cornwallis family. A native of Scotland, he was a prominent Halifax shipowner and merchant who had served in the British Army during the American Revolution.

Part of the island is known as Deadman's Beach, possibly named for the British practice of hanging pirates and disobedient sailors on the island, tarring their bodies to preserve them, and leaving them for other sailors to view as a reminder to abide by military regulations. This practice continued until about 1815.

At the tip of MacNab's Island are two smaller islands: Big and Little Thrumcap. The word "thrum" is derived from an early style of sailor's cap. The caps were knitted using rough fabric that was made by inserting wasted yarn ends into canvas.

A lighthouse extending from a point off of McNab's Island. (NSARM)

Situated near Big Thrumcap is Harrigan Point. In 1866, the SS *England*, en route to New York, sailed into Halifax Harbour and requested permission to quarantine cholera victims on MacNab's Island. Two hundred and fifty victims of the cholera epidemic are buried at Harrigan Point.

Most of the residents of MacNab's Island fished, farmed, or raised sheep. As early as 1872, lots on the island were being sold for cottages. Given its strategic position, fortifications were built on MacNab's Island throughout the 1800s. The Sherbrooke Martello Tower was constructed in 1814 and it became a lighthouse in 1828. Ives Point Battery, erected in 1865, was not completed until 1870. Fort MacNab was built between 1889 and 1891. A second fort, named Fort Hugonin after the husband of one of MacNab's daughters, was erected in 1899.

The military significance of MacNab's Island continued until the end of World War Two. Today much of the island's fortifications are being restored and tours to the island are available.

Devil's Island

This small island, situated near MacNab and Lawlor Islands, was once a thriving fishing community. As early as 1711, a Frenchman by the name of DeLabat lived on the island called "Isle Vert" or Green Island. Like many other early settlements, the island finally took on the name of the family that had settled there. DeLabat was eventually anglicized to "Deval" or "Devol," which evolved to become known as Devil's Island. Stories retold in Halifax state that Devil's Island is believed to be haunted, but this urban legend owes its origins to the anglicized version of the island's name.

A lighthouse keeper's home stands alone on Devil's Island in 1979. (NSARM)

Ben Henneberry and his son Edmund making cod liver oil on Devil's Island. (NSARM)

The first lifeboat station in Nova Scotia was established on Devil's Island in 1882, consisting of one large dory that was manned by the first operator, Benjamin Faulkner. The station took part in the rescue of many fishermen before it was disassembled fifty-five years later.

A number of families from Eastern Passage moved to the island, including those named Henneberry, Faulkner, Myers, and Naugler. By 1900, sixteen families called

Devil's Island home, among them ten with the surname of Henneberry. There were sixteen houses, one school, and two lighthouses. The islanders would row over to Eastern Passage to attend church services.

Twenty-eight families were living on the island by the 1920s, most engaged in successful fishery enterprises. The fishermen made cod-liver oil and other fish-related by-products. Unfortunately, the development of motorboats affected island life. Some families returned to Eastern Passage to live and motored out to their fishing spots. Their lives were also disrupted by a naval presence in Halifax and the continual passage of ships in and out of the harbour.

By 1967, settlement on the island was just about over. That year an automatic beacon made the lighthouse keeper redundant. The fishery was in decline and many of the island's young people were returning to the mainland to live and work.

Lawlor's Island

This small island is located at the mouth of Halifax Harbour, near MacNab's Island, and across from Eastern Passage. In 1750 it was known as Bloss's Island after Captain Thomas Bloss who received one of the earliest land grants. By 1758, it was called Webb's Island, then Carroll's Island in 1792, McNamara Island in 1821, Duggan's Island in 1829, and later Warren's Island. Today it is known as Lawlor's Island for one of its first settlers, James Lawlor. A quarantine hospital was also constructed on this island in 1866 to care for victims of cholera and other communicable diseases. It was expanded in 1872 and was eventually demolished when it was no longer needed.

Lawlor's Island as viewed from the fisherman's wharf in Eastern Passage. 1999 (AW)

Dartmouth

In 1750, the ship *Alderney* arrived with 353 immigrants. The Council at Halifax decided that these new arrivals should be settled on the other side of Halifax Harbour, in an area known to the Mi'kmaq as "Boon-amoogwaddy" or Tomcod Ground. The community was given the English name of Dartmouth in honour of William Legge, the 1st Earl of Dartmouth and a former nobleman in the court of Queen Anne.

By 1752, 53 families consisting of 193 people lived in the small community. In February of that year, the Connor family of Dartmouth started a ferry service. It was a large rowboat with sails, and passengers were summoned by a crew-member blowing on a conch shell. Improvements were made in 1816 with the arrival of the *Sherbrooke*, a 20-meter boat, powered by eight horses harnessed to iron stanchions that rotated the propeller sending the boat forward. The horses rested if the winds were favourable and sails could be raised. Samuel Cunard of the Cunard Shipping Lines managed to convince the city fathers in 1830 to trade in the horses for a steam-driven ferry. Ferries still criss-cross the harbour, but completion of the Angus L. Macdonald Bridge in 1955 provided an alternate means of travelling between the two cities.

Dartmouth developed slowly. In 1785, at the end of the American Revolution, a group of Quakers from Nantucket arrived in Dartmouth to set up a whaling trade. They built homes, a Quaker meeting house, a wharf for their vessels, and a factory to produce spermaceti candles and other products made from whale oil and carcasses. It was a profitable venture and many local residents were employed by the Quakers, but within ten years, around 1795, the whalers moved their operation to Wales.

The oldest structure in Dartmouth is the house of William Ray, one of the whalers. It is located at 59 Ochterloney Street and is believed to have been built around 1785 or 1786. Today it is a museum, furnished as a typical modest dwelling of a merchant of that time. Costumed guides are available for tours.

Other families soon arrived in the village of Dartmouth. The Hartshorne family, Loyalists who arrived in 1785, received a grant that included land that today comprises Portland, King, and Wentworth Streets.

By the early 1800s, Dartmouth consisted of about twenty-five families. Within twenty years, there were sixty houses, a church, gristmill, shipyards, sawmill, two inns and a bakery located near the harbour. In 1860, Starr Manufacturing Company was situated near the Shubenacadie Canal. The factory employed over 150 workers and manufactured ice skates, cut nails, vault doors, iron bridge work and other heavy iron products. The Mott's candy and soap factory, employing 100, opened at Hazelhurst. Consumer Cordage, a rope factory on Wyse Road, offered work to over 300, and the Symonds Foundry employed a further 50 to 100 people.

A ferry docked at the Dartmouth ferry terminal in 1942. (NSARM)

The first Natal Day Rowing Regatta took place in Dartmouth in August 1897. (NSARM)

The people of Dartmouth have celebrated Dartmouth's Natal Day since August 1895. The original idea was to celebrate the arrival of the railway but construction of the railroad tracks was incomplete on the appointed day. Since all the preparations for the festivities were ready, organizers decided to go ahead with a celebration of the town's birthday instead.

In 1941, the Dartmouth Natal Committee decided to erect a cairn in honour of the spirit and courage of the first settlers to Dartmouth's shore. It is situated in Leighton Dillman Park, part of common lands left to the community by the Quakers, and overlooks the harbour where the first settlers built their homes. It stands three meters high and is made of rocks gathered from Martinique Beach. A plaque in front of the cairn is inscribed with information describing the arrival of the "Alderney on August 12th, 1750 with 353 settlers."

As the population grew, more houses were erected and new businesses were established. Subdivisions such as Woodlawn, Woodside and Westphal developed on the outskirts of the town. Woodlawn was once part of the land purchased by a Loyalist, named Ebenezer Allen who became a prominent Dartmouth businessman. In 1786, he donated land near his estate to be used as a cemetery. Many early settlers are interred in the Woodlawn cemetery including the remains of the "Babes in the Woods," two sisters who wandered into the forest and perished.

Rod Morash founder of the Woodlawn Dairy delivers milk to his customers throughout the town of Dartmouth in 1910. (NSARM)

Westphal was named for two brothers, Philip and George, who were born on the old Preston Road. During the 1790s both boys left home to join the navy, eventually becoming British admirals.

Land in the Woodside district was purchased in the early 1800s by the Honorable John E. Fairbanks. His estate on Eastern Passage Road sloped down to the harbour. He constructed a cottage in which his family resided for many years. It became known as Woodside for the flower gardens and trees that adorned his garden. After Fairbanks's death, the property was sold several times and a number of commercial buildings were constructed in its place, including a sugar refinery and the Mount Hope Asylum, now known as the Nova Scotia Hospital.

In 1955, the Angus L. Macdonald Bridge was opened. The bridge, named in honour of a former premier of the province, gave families greater access to the Dartmouth side of the harbour. New homes, businesses and factories were constructed in the growing town. In 1961, some of the smaller communities that bordered Dartmouth officially amalgamated with it, creating the city of Dartmouth. Dartmouth's population doubled in the next ten years as boundaries were extended farther and as new residents and businesses arrived following the opening of the A. Murray Mackay Bridge across the Narrows in 1969. In 1996, the City of Dartmouth became a part of the Halifax Regional Municipality.

A general view of Halifax Harbour during the early 1890s with the Dartmouth shore in the foreground. (NSARM)

Eastern Passage

On the eastern side of Halifax Harbour is the small former community of Eastern Passage. It gets its name from the body of water, also known as Eastern Passage, that flows between MacNab's Island and the community. Once a Mi'kmaq summer campsite, the community has been settled over the years by French, British, and German pioneers. In 1754, a battery was constructed near Eastern Passage Road, called Fort Clarence to protect the inhabitants as they built houses away from the main part of the town.

The first land grant was issued to Joseph Gorham, shortly after 1750. Joseph and his three brothers, all from Massachusetts, were part of the Gorham Rangers, a military group comprised of mercenaries and a few Mohawk Indian allies. Joseph never settled on his lands, and his property was granted in 1798 to Jacaob Horne, a German who arrived from Quebec. Not long after Horne's arrival, other families received grants in the area, including those with the names of Naugle, Romkey, and Hartlen. Many of the families were farmers who crossed the harbour by ferry to sell their produce at the Halifax city market located at Cheapside.

The community developed slowly. During the mid-1800s, only twenty-six families settled there. Within the next twenty-five years, seventy-five more families arrived and the 1871 census lists families by the name of Horne, Cleary, Moser, Edward, Conrad, Henneberry, and Welshman. Some were descendants of the Foreign Protestant settlers of Lunenburg County. As the population of the settlement continued to increase, the people of this community became a close-knit group. Most small communities have central meeting places where residents can meet and talk about the day's events—usually a general store or local post office. The people of Eastern Passage were no exception. For many years they would meet at Quigley's General Store.

Walking along the boardwalk at Fisherman's Cove in Eastern Passage. 1999 (AW)

The location of the community was strategic during wartime, an important factor during both the First and Second World Wars. The fear of an enemy attack on the harbour, where convoys bound for Europe gathered, was very real. Eastern Passage, at the extreme outer edge of the eastern side of Halifax Harbour, was ideally suited for a defense system. An American air base was established at Baker's Point. During the Second World War this became Canadian Forces Base Shearwater. Today the base includes a Canadian Forces Helicopter Squadron and a civilian airport. Near the entrance is the Shearwater Aviation Museum, located at 13 Bonaventure Avenue, where visitors can examine the numerous exhibits and the collection of aircrafts on display depicting the history of the Canadian Maritime Military Aviation. Farther along, on the shoreline, is Fisherman's Cove, a restored 200-year old fishing village that provides insight into the historical past of a fisherman's life. There are shops selling local crafts, dining facilities, and a boardwalk where visitors and residents can walk along the shoreline, watching fishermen unload their catch.

Richard Hartlin of South East Passage near Hartlin's Point with a house in the background believed to be haunted. (NSARM)

Cow Bay

Cow Bay, on Highway #207, about 13 kilometers south east of Dartmouth and to the west of Cole Harbour, was named for Robert Cowie who, with Roger Hill received a land grant in the area in 1763. By 1772, Charles Palmer and Richard Monday had also settled in the community.

In the 1840s, gold was discovered by Al Negus, but it was not mined until fifty years later. Other minerals, including graphite and lead, were also discovered and the gold mining rights were turned over to an American company.

In the 1850s, the beach, which extends for a one and one-half kilometers along the coast, became a popular summer resort for the residents

Cow Bay Beach today where swimmers and sunbathers enjoy the cool ocean waters while children create castles in the sand. 1999 (AW)

The Bronnum moose sculpture overlooking Cow Bay Beach is still being enjoyed by children. 1999 (AW)

of Dartmouth and the surrounding communities. By 1860, local landowners recognized the economic advantages that could be made by renting rooms to visitors in the Cow Bay area. In the 1930s, a dance hall and canteen were built and families from Halifax, Dartmouth, and the surrounding communities travelled to Silver Sands Beach, one of the finest in the province. A local sculptor, Winston Bronnum, made the beach famous when he placed various animal sculptures on the sandy beach for the enjoyment of the children. His sculpture of a moose was placed at the entrance to the beach. Other animal sculptures followed, including a turtle, seal, whale, and alligator, but only the moose remains.

Unfortunately, the Silver Sands Beach, or Cow Bay Beach as some people call it, was being destroyed. Sand was being removed to fill in the container piers along the harbourside and to build the runway at Shearwater Airport. Removal of sand left the beaches vulnerable to the erosion of the tides and so the Provincial Government decided to step in and pass legislation to protect the material on beaches from removal.

COLE HARBOUR

A few years after Dartmouth was founded in 1750, Governor Charles Lawrence decided to have a road constructed to the township that would eventually bear his name. Houses appeared along the road and soon news reached the Foreign Protestant settlers in the Lunenburg area that rich farmland could be found to the east of Dartmouth. Several families moved to the region, where they were joined by New England settlers and later by the United Empire Loyalists who arrived from the United States after the American revolution.

Cole Harbour Road prior to becoming a two lane paved highway. (NSARM)

The area they settled was known to the Mi'kmaq as "Wonpaak," which means "still water" or "white water." The English name may refer to an early pioneer family, though in a land grant of 1765 it is called Coal Harbour.

Present-day Cole Harbour Road. (AW)

The community was originally part of a grant issued to Benjamin Green Jr. in 1765. Others who settled in the area included families with the surnames of Beck, Bissett, Conrad, Gammon, Turner, Morash and Settle, many of whom have descendants still residing in the area.

Among the earliest settlers was Thomas Beamish, grandfather of Dr. Thomas Beamish Akins who wrote an early history of Halifax. In 1782, George Bissett (Bizette) and George Harper both received 600-acre grants. The Bissett family built the first oat mill in the community. By 1830, the Gammon family arrived and were renowned for their finely designed furniture. Toolmaker James Beck also resided in the area and made the ploughs and other farm implements needed to cultivate the land.

One enterprising group of settlers established the Cole Harbour Dyke Company in 1842 with the intention of cultivating marshland. Two Englishmen worked on the project: George Crawley was hired to construct the dyke while John Watson was taken on as the civil engineer. After five years the venture failed.

Undeterred, a second attempt was made in 1876. This time, James VanBuskirk of Dartmouth and two Englishmen—Thomas Watson, a mining engineer and John Watson, the civil engineer during the first attempt—purchased lands around the harbour. They eventually managed to construct the dyke despite the deaths of several workers. But the company was in debt and the land was sold at a public auction. Many others purchased the land over the years, the last being Peter MacNab Kuhn, descendant of one of the families who arrived with Governor Cornwallis in 1749.

In 1973, the Cole Harbour Rural Heritage Society was formed to preserve the area's heritage. The Society operates the popular Cole Harbour Farm Museum at 471 Popular Drive. The land, located today in an urban setting, was owned by a number of families over the years, including those with the names of Hartshorne, Turner, Settle, and Harris. On the property is the Giles Saltbox House, one of the oldest buildings in Cole Harbour, built around 1804 or earlier. Joseph Giles bought the land on which the house was originally situated from Jacob Conrad in 1789, and it remained in the Giles family until 1971. It was then moved by the Nova Scotia Housing Commission to its present location at the Cole Harbour Farm Museum in 1976.

Today many of the old farmsteads have gone. Now the community is a large residential subdivision. Bel-Ayr was established in 1959. By 1970, Colby Village had been developed. It was followed by the Forest Hills subdivision a year later.

The Giles Saltbox House now part of the Cole Harbour Heritage Farm Museum. 1999 (AW)

The Cole Harbour Parks and Trails Association along with the Cole Harbour Rural Heritage Society joined forces to achieve park status for the salt marshes found within the area of the Trans Canada Trail project being developed around the Cole Harbour area. In 1998 the association was successful in acquiring their objective of full park status. They are now in the process of developing the abandoned railway lines as public trails in the hopes of increasing tourism, thus the economy as well.

Rainbow Haven Beach is located at the mouth of Cole Harbour. This popular beach is ideal for walking, hiking, picnicking, and bird-watching as well as fishing and sketching. It also can be used for canoeing, swimming, and boating. Clam-digging is also possible at low tide during the cool months.

Percy Conrod riding on a railway trolley, which was converted from a pumper known as the Casey Jones, over the Cole Harbour dykes in 1923. (HRM)

Chapter Two

BEDFORD/ SACKVILLE AREA

- Rockingham
- Prince's Lodge
- Birch Cove
- Bedford
- Lower, Middle, and Upper Sackville, Lakeview
- Beaverbank
- Kinsac

A photograph of the Rotunda, former music room and only structure remaining of the Wentworth estate, taken in 1953. (NSARM)

This chapter explores settlement along the shores of the Bedford Basin and the communities that developed along the road to Windsor.

As soon as he had established a fort at Halifax in 1749, Governor Edward Cornwallis saw a need for the construction of a road from the garrison and around the bay to connect Halifax with the English-speaking settlements along the Minas Basin near Windsor. To protect the road workers, he commissioned John Gorham of Massachusetts and his Rangers to build Fort Sackville at the head of Bedford Basin. (Although the nearby community was called Bedford in honour of John Russell, the 4th Duke of Bedford and Secretary of State for the colonies in 1749, it continued to be known locally as Sackville until construction of the railroad in the mid-1850s.)

With protection from the garrison at Fort Sackville and with the roadway constructed, new communities soon developed in this region.

ROCKINGHAM

Rockingham is located on the west side of the Bedford Basin, about six-and-a-half kilometers from Halifax. Until about 1886, the area was known as "Four Mile House District" because of its distance from Halifax. As the community grew, it became known as Rockingham after the social club Sir John Wentworth had started at Prince's Lodge on his estate.

Mount St. Vincent University in 1873, during the time it was a college for young ladies. (NSARM)

One of the first establishments in the area was the Rockingham Inn, built around 1800. The Evans family once owned the inn and was descended from one of the first pioneer families to settle in Halifax.

For many years the inn remained a popular gathering spot for military officers and prominent members of Halifax's leading families who wanted to discuss literary matters. They included the Strachan, Boak, Parker, and Howe families. In 1841, the old wooden structure caught fire and burned to the ground.

Mount St. Vincent University, which overlooks Bedford Basin, was built in 1873 in Rockingham. The college was established by the Sisters of Charity as a residential Catholic school for young ladies. It became a college in 1925 and was proclaimed a university in 1966. Although most of its students are female undergraduates, the university has been co-educational since 1966.

Following the development of a subdivision in 1962, the Rockingham community has become largely residential, with its residents commuting to work in Halifax or Dartmouth. Like many other communities on the outskirts of Halifax, Rockingham was amalgamated with the city on January 1, 1969. The history of the area is being compiled by the Rockingham Historical Society for the benefit of future generations.

Prince's Lodge

Many estates were constructed along the shore of the Bedford Basin. One estate of particular note was part of a grant issued to William Foy in 1772; he was one of Governor Edward Cornwallis' captains. The estate covered an area from where the Bicentennial Highway is now located to the shores of the Bedford Basin. Captain Foy sold the land to John Willis who in turn sold it to John Lawrence. Eventually Sir John Wentworth purchased it from Lawrence and permitted him to reside in a small stone building located on the property that was called "Friar Lawrence's Cell."

In 1794, His Royal Highness Prince Edward, Duke of Kent, arrived to serve in Halifax. Accompanying him was his French mistress Julie St. Laurent. The Duke was often entertained at the "Friar's Cell" and liked it so much that Wentworth felt obliged to offer it to him during his stay in Halifax. Prince Edward accepted, renovated the residence and brought in landscapers from England to develop the gardens around the estate. The result was what is today Hemlock Ravine Park, 185 acres with a heart shaped pond, known as Julie's Pond and constructed by the Duke in honour of his mistress, Julie St. Laurent.

When Prince Edward returned to England, the Wentworths resumed living in the lodge, now called the Prince's Lodge. It was here that Sir

John established the Rockingham Club. But after Sir John died, the estate was neglected. By 1870, in ruins, it was sold at auction and divided into building lots, although residential housing did not emerge until after World War Two.

A painting of Governor Wentworth's estate which became known as Prince's Lodge. (NSARM)

All that remains of the original estate is the Rotunda. This is a small, round music room that stands on a knoll overlooking Bedford Basin. It was supposedly one of Julie St. Laurent's favourite spots. In 1959, the Rotunda was acquired by the Provincial Government. Today it is privately owned and a designated Provincially Registered Heritage Property.

The Prince's Lodge area now consists mainly of residential homes and a few commercial enterprises.

Birch Cove

Birch Cove, on the Bedford Highway just eight kilometers northwest of Halifax, was used by the Mi'kmaq as a summer camping ground until the 1920s. There are also traces of an early Acadian village on the cove. A gravesite, uncovered in 1890, was at first thought to be a Mi'kmaq burial site or perhaps the graves of some of the French sailors who had died aboard the Duc D'Anville's French fleet. However, thirty graves were dug up and scientific analysis of the remains proved that they were Acadians settlers.

One of the first English-speaking settlers was William Donaldson, who named his estate Birch Cove after the birch trees that overhung the cove. Others who settled in the community around 1835 included families by the names of Goff, Ryan, Maxwell, Doyle, Quigley, Beckwith, Hopewell, and Strickland. By 1930, those living around the cove included the Gifford, Cosgrove, Holmes, and Brewster families.

Birch Cove, like Rockingham, was amalgamated with the city of Halifax on January 1, 1969.

Bedford

Soon after establishing the garrison at Halifax, Governor Cornwallis organized his men and began the construction of a road leading to the Minas Bay on the Bay of Fundy using Mi'kmaq footpaths as their guide. To protect the route and the road workers, he hired John Gorham and his Rangers to erect a defense post at the head of the Bedford Basin. It was named Fort Sackville after Lionel Cranfield, Viscount Sackville and first Duke of Dorset. The area around the fort became known as Sackville until the mid-1850s, when it became better known as Bedford.

The boundary lines for the community of Sackville were eventually placed further along the Bedford Highway beyond the Basin. Then the highway, the basin, and the village at the head of the Bedford Basin took on the name of Bedford in honour of John Russell, the 4th Duke of Bedford and Secretary of State for the colonies in 1749. The name became official during the construction of the railway in the mid-1850s.

In 1752, George Scott was among the first to receive a large land grant in the Fort Sackville area. Joseph Scott, paymaster at the Halifax Garrison from 1761 to 1763 received two grants: one in 1759 and a further one hundred acres in 1765. In 1770 he built Scott Manor House on his estate abutting Fort Sackville. Today the mansion is a Provincial designated heritage property.

By the 1780s, more settlers had arrived and the road that Cornwallis had built was well used. Then in 1782 a toll-gate was erected. The residents were not pleased to have to pay a fee to travel along the road, so one night, under cover of darkness, several horsemen gathered to destroy the gate. A reward was offered to anyone with information leading to the arrest of the vandals, but no one stepped forward. A new gate was built, but it too was torn down in 1785—this time never replaced.

A photograph of a painting by Robert Petley of Bedford Basin ca. 1835. (Courtesy of the National Archives of Canada, C-115424)

Eventually, other families arrived and set up small businesses. After receiving a 245-acre land grant, the Mixner family carried on a tannery business for a number of years prior to 1813. Around 1819, Anthony Holland established the Acadian Paper Mill on the Basin to provide paper to produce the *Acadian Recorder*, a Halifax newspaper. Flemming Smith, the son of Virginian slaves, sold spruce, hop, and corn to Halifax merchants. He also established picnic grounds for those people who wanted to come and enjoy the spectacular beauty of Bedford Basin and the surrounding countryside.

In 1836, William Piers erected a gristmill where the Hammonds Plains Road meets the Bedford Highway. At the time he had a land grant on property then known as Lower Bedford or Millview. After the death of William Piers, his heirs sold the property in 1866 to a Halifax merchant, William Hare. In 1876 it was again sold, this time to William C. Moir.

Fort Sackville Barracks located at the head of the Bedford Basin in 1878. (NSARM)

The Moir family business began in Halifax manufacturing bakery products. In 1873, a son of William Moir, James, added confectionery goods to their business. Eventually the Moirs, Son and Co. moved a part of their business to the Bedford property. The Moirs Mill generating station is the only building left standing that was once a part of the Moirs Mill factory. Built in the early 1930s, it supplied the necessary electricity required to operate the factory as it produced chocolates and wooden boxes. The structure was the first property in Bedford to be designated as a Provincial heritage property. Today the building is used as a Visitor's Information Centre.

During the early 1800s, the area became known as Piers Mill after William Piers. It had had other names: Nine Mile River, Lower Bedford, Doyle's Dump, and even "The Dump." When the railway went through the station at Piers Mill it was renamed Millview—a reflection on the number of mills in the area. In 1896 the name became official by an Act of Legislation. Today it has been amalgamated into the town of Bedford.

A number of establishments were built for travellers looking for an

The Moir's mill generating station built during the 1930s, near the entrance to the Hammond's Plains Road. 1999 (AW)

Sailing on the Bedford Basin, 1999 (AW)

overnight stop on their way to the Annapolis Valley. One, the Florence Hotel in Millview, was built in 1896. It was later named the Rockaway Inn but unfortunately in 1931 it burned to the ground and was not rebuilt.

On July 1, 1980, Bedford was incorporated as a town. It is now part of the greater Halifax Regional Municipality.

LOWER, MIDDLE, AND UPPER SACKVILLE

Sackville received its name from Lionel Cranfield, Viscount Sackville, and his name is connected to Fort Sackville.

The Mi'kmaq name for the area was called "Aloosoolawakade" meaning "a place of measles," a disease that ravaged the early settlements and caused the deaths of many settlers as well as numerous Mi'kmaq.

The first known land grants were awarded to settlers along the Windsor Road, a footpath well travelled by Acadians and Mi'kmaqs prior to the building of the British garrison in 1749. William Fenerty, an Irishman, received a land grant in 1784 and operated the Springfield Inn from 1802 until 1821. His grandson, Charles Fenerty, is famous for having discovered how to produce paper from spruce wood pulp, thereby replacing the rag paper mill established in 1819 by Anthony Holland. His process was made public in 1844.

Herman A. Fultz of Lower Sackville. (NSARM)

Dr. Abraham Gesner, discoverer of kerosene, was a resident for several short periods of time. Dr. George Lawson, who developed a botanical garden of rare and unusual plants at his Lucyfield farm, lived in the area during the 1860s. The poet

Kenneth Leslie lived in and wrote about the Sackville community. William Fultz, who built his home at the junction of the Windsor and Cobequid Roads in 1865, named it Ten Mile House because of the distance it lay from the town of Halifax. Today the Fultz house is a museum dedicated to preserving and depicting the unique cultural heritage of the Sackville community.

The population of Sackville began to increase as more families moved to the suburbs in the 1950s. It tripled its size after becoming a "new town" in the 1970s. During the last twenty years, the population has reached the point that now the community is self-contained with

Fultz House Museum (formerly Ten Mile House) built ca. 1865 is located at the corner of the Cobequid Road and the former Windsor Road. 1999 (AW)

such amenities as shopping malls, businesses, schools, churches, and professional services.

The Sackville Historical Society continues to preserve the history and culture of the Sackville communities. Volunteers have compiled a collection of historical data on the families, houses and businesses. In

1995, the Royal Canadian Legion in Sackville erected a Cenotaph made of various stones from the seventy-three countries around the world where Canadian soldiers have fought and died to preserve world peace. The Cenotaph is located at the entrance to Lower Sackville in a prominent spot located in the Sackville Heritage Park.

There are two other communities within the general boundaries of the Sackville area. One is Lakeview, located on the north west side of Rocky Lake, over three kilometers from Lower Sackville. Lots overlooking the lake were sold in 1891 in the hopes that a town would be established, but the area has remained rural.

The second is the small former settlement of Maroon Hill. Following an insurrection in their homeland in 1796, Black Jamaicans, known as Maroons, came to Nova Scotia to establish their own community and to work on the Halifax fortifications under construction. The winters proved too harsh for people accustomed to warm Caribbean breezes and many petitioned the government for permission to sail in 1800 to the West African country of Sierra Leone. Those who remained were offered land in Sackville in an area that became known as Maroon Hill. Over time the small community has become a part of the town of Sackville.

Beaverbank

Northeast of Sackville, about twenty-five kilometers from Halifax, lies the village of Beaverbank.

One of the first residents was John Barnstead. He and his parents arrived in Nova Scotia as Loyalists from Boston in 1776. Two additional families arrived after the War of 1812—George and Robert Barrett, shopkeepers from Oxford, England. In 1813, land was granted to William Nicholson. Three years later, in 1816, the Fultz family (William, John, Anthony, George, and Daniel) received over one thousand acres.

By 1850, the village of Beaverbank was growing. Families such as Barrett, Peveril, Fleiger, McGrath, Dooley, Ross, Nicholson, Barnstead, and Hallisey, played significant roles in the development of the community and many of their descendants still reside in the area. Daniel Hallisey was the postmaster for many years and his family continued to operate the post office for a total of ninety-nine years until his granddaughter, Mary O'Driscoll, retired as postmistress in 1962 at the age of seventy-two.

During the 1960s, as the population of Halifax expanded, affordable land for housing on the peninsula became scarce. Many families chose to move farther away from the metropolitan area and villages such as Beaverbank were considered to be outskirts of the city of Halifax.

KINSAC

Kinsac is a tiny rural community on the west side of Lake Kinsac, approximately twenty kilometers from Halifax but still within the Bedford-Sackville district. The name may be derived from a Mi'kmaq word for "running water."

The settlement was originally considered a part of the village of Beaverbank and land granted in 1810 was issued to John Fleiger and John Pleasant. But after the railway was constructed towards the end of the last century, Kinsac developed on its own as a separate community. Today it remains a rural community with cottages used year-round for hunting and fishing.

The Nelson family who resided in Kinsac during the 1950s. (NSARM)

Chapter Three

Preston to Conrod Settlement

- Preston, North/East Preston
- Upper, West, and East Lawrencetown
- Minesville
- Montague Gold Mines
- Porter's Lake/West Porter's Lake
- Seaforth
- Three Fathom Harbour/Lower Three Fathom Harbour
- Grand Desert
- Head of Chezzetcook/West/East Chezzetcook/Lower East Chezzetcook
- Conrod Settlement

Lawrencetown Beach on a hot summer afternoon with the surfers riding the ocean waves. 1999 (AW)

Introduction

The garrison at Halifax was still under construction, settled by soldiers, merchants, and artisans, when Charles Lawrence became Governor of Nova Scotia. He decided to explore the Eastern Shore region, northeast of the settlement of Dartmouth.

By 1753, he had decided to settle families in an area called "Muscodoboit" by the Mi'kmaq. This land included the town of Dartmouth and along the eastern shore to the Chezzetcook Acadian settlement. Today it is the area beyond Chezzetcook that is known as Musquodoboit. To encourage settlement, a road was built through the dense forest to the Township of Lawrencetown, named for the Governor.

The first land grants went to prominent Halifax officials, who built summer residences for themselves and their families. In time, these estates were divided into smaller lots and sold individually.

Other small communities soon sprang up along the shore as the road continued along the coast. Most were settled by immigrants who had arrived with Cornwallis in 1749. Some were Foreign Protestants who had first settled in the Lunenburg area and now decided to venture farther up the eastern coast where the land was more fertile. They were joined by a few of the original Acadian families who had been deported in 1755 and later returned, or who had hidden in the forests among their Mi'kmaq friends until a general amnesty was declared.

Today many of the farms along the coast have disappeared, replaced by subdivisions and commercial enterprises. Where once a narrow road wound its way, there is now a highway sweeping past many of these communities.

Preston, North Preston

Preston Township, established approximately thirteen kilometers northeast of Dartmouth, lies along old Highway #7.

In 1784, a surveyor, Theophilus Chamberlain, together with a number of Loyalists and disbanded soldiers, received a land grant within Halifax County's second township. Named for Preston, a town in Lancarshire, England, the community was soon settled by the Stayner, Greenwood, Allan, Smith, Russell, King, Wisdom, and Long families.

They were joined in 1796 by over five hundred "Maroons," Black Jamaicans deported from Jamaica after an insurrection and brought to Nova Scotia to work on the fortifications being erected around the city of Halifax. However they had difficulty adjusting to the cold Nova Scotia climate and sought permission to join other Blacks who some fifteen years earlier had founded the West African country of Sierra Leone.

Several "Maroon Families" did remain behind when the others departed in 1800. The Colleys stayed on Governor Wentworth's farm and today descendants of this family can still be found residing in the

East Preston area. The descendants are the relations of Sarah Colley, Wentworth's mistress, who had a son named George Wentworth Colley who was born in 1804 and died in 1893. He inherited the Governor's summer place located on the Colley farm in Preston.

Thomas Beal and his family in Cherry Brook. (NSARM)

More Black refugees arrived in Nova Scotia following the War of 1812 on British warships. Offered the land vacated by the Maroons, these families were allocated narrow lots leading down to a lake. In time, a road was built to give the settlers easier access to and from their homes, nevertheless, the town of North Preston remained landlocked as late as the 1970s.

William Riley and his daughter Rose on the doorstep in Cherry Brook in 1947. (NSARM)

Originally all of Preston Township was landlocked, although it was surrounded by three lakes—Porter's Lake, Lake Major and Lake Loon—each with its own settlement. To the east of Lake Major lay the area known as "New Road," named for the road constructed shortly after the area was first settled. Those who lived along the road soon became part of the Preston community.

The land offered to the Black settlers was rocky, tree covered, and generally infertile. The refugees struggled with boulders and tree stumps to cultivate their land to produce vegetables for home consumption or to sell at city markets. Some of the men augmented their income by trapping small animals, raising hogs, or planting potatoes. It was subsistence farming. In time, the community population began to decline as younger generations sought different kinds of work.

Former home of the Colley family located on the original site of the Wentworth family's Preston estate ca. 1930. (NSARM)

By the 1850s, many of the Black settlers of Preston Township chose to relocate to other established Black communities, such as Africville, Hammonds Plains, or Beechville, as well as to Windsor in Hants County. The community continued to decrease in size as people sought work elsewhere. In 1901, several families emigrated to Boston, Massachusetts, while in the 1960s many moved to other parts of Canada, such as Montreal and Toronto. However Statistics Canada's records show that the population increased significantly between 1951 and 1981 as housing and transportation improved. Now many of those who live in Preston commute to Halifax or Dartmouth for work, entertainment, and recreation.

Several other small communities have evolved near the Preston area. Cherry Brook, named for its cherry trees, developed along the southwest shore of Lake Major. At the corner of Cherry Brook Road and Highway #7, is the Black Cultural Centre. It was established in the 1980s to preserve the history and culture of the Black people who settled in Nova Scotia. The Centre includes exhibits and information on community life, religious beliefs, military service, migration routes, and the family histories of some of those Black settlers from Preston and surrounding districts.

Not far from Preston is the community of Lake Echo, which received its name because of the acoustics which cause echoes of sound to travel across the lake. The first land grant of three hundred acres was given to Alexander Taylor in 1818, who settled along the northeast side of the lake. Today the community consists of residential homes and various commercial enterprises.

A portrait photograph of Henry Francis Green, a son of Francis Green and a descendant of one of the original settlers of Preston. (NSARM)

Upper, West, and East Lawrencetown

The area along the coast, east of Dartmouth was known to the Mi'kmaq as "Wampack, Taboolsimket," meaning "two small branches flowing through the sands." Long before European settlement, the Mi'kmaq set up their summer camps in the area while in winter they would move inland to hunt game in the forests. By the eighteenth century, they had been joined by a number of Acadian settlers with whom they traded.

Nova Scotia's Governor Charles Lawrence, mindful of the threat the French posed at Fortress Louisbourg on Cape Breton Island and of the intentions of the Mi'kmaq and the Acadians, decided to populate this area with hard-working Protestant families. In 1754, he offered land grants to twenty such families, who referred to their settlement as Lawrence's town, which quickly became Lawrencetown.

Lawrencetown settlers felt isolated and within a few years many had returned to the security of Halifax. By 1763, only three families remained in Lawrence's town.

Halifax businessman Benjamin Green, Jr. continued to live on his land grant which covered what today is West Lawrencetown, all of East Lawrencetown, Conrod's Beach, Three Fathom Harbour, and the land along the coast of West Chezzetcook. After his death, his widow Suzanne and their thirteen children divided his property among themselves. His son, Richard, received the land around Conrod Beach while his brothers Joseph and Henry and his two sisters Susan and Elizabeth remained in the Lawrencetown area. Susan married Captain Samuel Parker and members of the Green and Parker family descendants still live in the community and surrounding areas.

Captain Parker, a war hero, perished in the Crimean War, far from his family in Lawrencetown. His exploits have been commemorated with a memorial at the entrance to the Old Burying Grounds, St. Paul's Cemetery, located on Barrington Street in Halifax. A lion atop a cenotaph honours the courage displayed by Captain Parker and his compatriot, Major Welsford.

By 1827, about 161 people had settled in the Lawrencetown area, including the Green, Lloyd, Crowell, Crook, Wiseman, Shaw, Pentz, and

The Parker-Welsford Memorial or Sebastopol Monument erected in St. Paul's Cemetery, Halifax in honor of two young men who lost their lives in the Crimean War (ca. 1863-1873)

Wood families. Over the next ten years, they were joined by Irish, Scottish, and German families, with such names as Murphy, Settle, Conrad (Conrod), Leslie, Taylor, Moors, McKenna, and Sellar. By 1860, there were the Gammon, Bissett, Robinson, Giles, Morash, and Lawlor families also living in the Lawrencetown area.

Most families fished for a living, though some were quite inventive at turning marsh into farming land. By 1910, a community agricultural society was established.

As more families were drawn to the Eastern Shore, the area was divided into Upper and Lower Lawrencetown. Today there are three distinct areas—Upper, West, and East Lawrencetown—though most people equate the community with Lawrencetown Beach Provincial Park and a nearby interpretive centre. It's a popular place for swimming and surfing, and even in the depths of winter you may catch sight of a surfer or two.

Minesville

This rural community, at the head of Lawrencetown Lake off Highway #7, is typical of a number of similar villages along the Eastern Shore that developed in the mid-1800s with the discovery of gold. In the 1860s the area became prosperous, but within ten years the gold was gone and the prospectors had departed. For awhile the community was a prosperous lumbering district but as more trees were felled, the operations ground slowly to a halt. Today, Minesville is an area of new forest growth and is popular with weekend cottagers.

Montague Gold Mines

Montague Gold Mines, like Minesville, draws its name from the discovery of gold, this time by prospector Ben Clarke in 1863.

The community's origins go back to the Honorable Charles Morris, Surveyor-General of Nova Scotia, who received a land grant not long after the Loyalists began to arrive in Nova Scotia in the early 1780s. With the help of the local young people, Mr. Morris built a summer home on a 900-acre estate to the east of Lake Loon. The home remained in the Morris family for many years.

In 1845, retired Lieutenant Colonel George F. Thompson of the Royal Engineers bought the residence. He arrived with his wife, children, and an invalid aunt who died shortly afterwards and was buried in the Catholic Cemetery on Geary Street. The burial startled residents who knew the good Colonel to be an Anglican. Nothing was done, however, until military officers who had known the family while they resided in Barbados arrived in Halifax and realized something was amiss.

An order was given to exhume the body and hold an inquest. Then the true story came out. The aunt was Catherine Thompson, the Colonel's wife. The family had lived through an insurrection in Barbados during which Catherine had witnessed the murder of her baby son. Unable to deal with such horror, she went insane. Meanwhile, the Thompson's housekeeper Mary Taylor, the widow of one of Colonel Thompson's sergeants, suggested that she would care for Catherine if the Colonel would treat her as his wife. The family then moved to Nova Scotia, hoping the hoax would never be discovered. After the story came out, Catherine's body was returned to Geary Cemetery.

The old Morris Lake Loon house changed hands again in 1847; it was purchased by Colonel George Montague after the Thompsons left for unknown parts. The settlement remained small until the discovery of gold in the 1860s. After the mines were depleted a few years later, the community turned to lumbering and farming. Today, Montague Gold Mines is a small residential area with easy access to Dartmouth.

Porter's Lake/West Porter's Lake

The Mi'kmaq called the area around Porter's Lake "Amaguncheech," meaning "a little breezy place." When William Porter and other Loyalists, including the Black, Watson, Clinton, Armstrong, and Bates families, received a land grant in 1784, it was known as Maryville. By 1790, William Porter had built a sawmill at the head of the lake to harvest the trees from the dense forest and today the community and the lake are named for him.

Like many nearby communities, Porter's Lake enjoyed a brief period of prosperity with the discovery of gold during the late 1800s on Thompson's Hill, on the eastern shore, now called West Porter's Lake.

The lake is a beautiful spot, favoured by hunters, fishermen, and other water sports enthusiasts. At the Old Hall Wilderness Heritage Centre, located in Porter's Lake at 4694 Highway #7, visitors can explore the connection between the community and the wilderness, with displays that depict the region's natural beauty, vibrant community life, industry and recreational opportunities.

Porter's Lake is one of the largest lakes located in the HRM area. 1999 (AW)

Farmland can still be found in the small community of Seaforth. 1999 (AW)

SEAFORTH

The Seaforth community is situated between Lawrencetown and West Chezzetcook, on Highway #207. In 1779, Seaforth was a part of the Township of Lawrencetown and laid out to receive German settlers. Among those who acquired land grants were Captains Taggart and Spike. Later the community became a part of Three Fathom Harbour. Then, around 1870, villagers renamed it Seaforth because it reminded them of a town in England of the same name

THREE FATHOM HARBOUR/ LOWER THREE FATHOM HARBOUR

The origin of the name of the fishing village known as Three Fathom Harbour is derived from the depth of its harbour; at high tide the harbour is no more than three fathoms (about six meters) deep. Situated at the head of the harbour, along Highway #207, about sixteen kilometers from Dartmouth, this piece of land was first granted in 1779 to Captain Taggart of Seaforth and to James Graham, an Irishman who was known to be residing in the area as late as 1792. Within thirty-five years, twelve families were settled in the community. Nearby are salt marshes, the nesting grounds of numerous salt water birds.

Crossing the bridge over the Three Fathom River. 1999 (AW)

GRAND DESERT

The Grand Desert community is located on the west side of Chezzetcook Inlet. In some ways the area resembles a large sandy desert. Sand washed in by the ocean surf has contributed to its appearance, though some people say that at one time the land was stripped of its trees and looked barren. Apparently Acadians used the word "desert" to indicate that the land was forested before being cleared by settlers.

The community was originally part of the Lawrencetown Township. In 1788, several local families petitioned the government for land, but they didn't receive ownership of their property until 1814.

Grand Desert's community store. 1999 (AW)

Among the first settlers were the families of John and Joseph LaPierre and Felix Wolfe. Joseph LaPierre was born in the Beaubassin area and after the Acadian expulsion in 1755, was imprisoned at Fort Beausejour for several years. Later he settled in Grand Desert. Augustine (Felix) Wolfe, originally from Alsace, France came to Halifax with settlers who accompanied Edward Cornwallis in 1749. For reasons unknown he chose to relocate among the Acadians at Grand Desert. Today descendants of all three families live in the area.

Head of Chezzetcook, West Chezzetcook, East Chezzetcook, Lower East Chezzetcook

Many stories abound about the origin of the name of these four small communities. The Mi'kmaq called the area "Chesetkook" or "Sesetkook," meaning "flowing rapidly in many channels." The French named the Inlet "Chez les coques," or "home of clams." Other spelling variations include "Sheyeticook" and "Chezekkouk." The four settlements surround Chezzetcook Inlet, about twenty-one kilometers from Dartmouth on Route #207.

Similar to Grand Desert, this was an Acadian community in the early 1700s, long before Halifax was founded. After the general expulsion of Acadians in 1755, many Acadians hid in the forests to escape deportation. Some people were captured by British forces; others returned on their own, around 1764. Among the imprisoned Acadians who eventually came to Chezzetcook was a man by the name of Boudrot (Boudreau). Born and raised in Port Royal (Annapolis Royal), Mr. Boudreau was captured trying to escape deportation and imprisoned at Fort Edward, near Windsor, Hants County. The Bellfontaine family from the Saint John River region of New Brunswick found themselves imprisoned in Halifax after their arrest, and also moved to the Chezzetcook area on their release. Other settlers who joined the Boudrots and Bellfontaines in the Chezzetcook area included the three Petitpas brothers from Port Toulouse, who arrived in 1760. Another, Jean Pierre Murphy (part Acadian and part Irish) arrived from Cape Breton in 1785. Simon Julien, who was born in Angouleme around 1783, jumped ship in Halifax in 1805. He settled in Chezzetcook after being told there were Acadian families living in the region.

Loyalists also settled in the Chezzetcook area. Many were of German background and included families with the names of Conrod (Conrad), Meisner, Gaetz (Gates), Webber, Crawford, and Myers. Others were of French, English, Irish, or Scottish origins, with such names as Fillis, Leslie, Ferguson, Romans, Myatts, and Smith.

Today, many of the families residing in the Chezzetcook communities are descendants of these original Acadian and Loyalist settlers. The Chezzetcook Historical Society is compiling family histories of early settlers to preserve the culture of the people of the communities surrounding the Chezzetcook Inlet.

Mrs. Lewis Romo, aged 104 sitting in front of her home in West Chezzetcook. (NSARM)

Conrod Settlement

George Conrod (Conrad) epitomized Governor Edward Cornwallis's intentions in the British colony of Nova Scotia. He was born on Corkum's Island, Lunenburg County, in 1756, the son of Jacob and Elizabeth Conrod. They were among the Foreign Protestants of German descent who Cornwallis had brought to Nova Scotia to settle in the Lunenburg area to countermand the presence of a largely Catholic Acadian population in the region.

Matthew Conrod, a descendant of the original settlers of Conrod Settlement, standing in his hay field. (NSARM)

In 1812, George Conrod was granted land between Chezzetcook and Petpeswick Inlets. Then in 1818, he moved farther along the Chezzetcook Harbour and formed the community of Conrod Settlement with several other families. Located on Conrod Lake, less than thirty kilometers northeast of Dartmouth, the community still bears his name and is home to many of George Conrod's descendants.

A group of mill workers in front of the cook house in Conrod Settlement. L to R: Ervin, Milton, Arthur and Roland Conrod, James Lockyer, John Roast and Arthur Myers. (MRM)

Chapter Four

PETPESWICK/ DEBAIE'S COVE

- West Petpeswick, East Petpeswick
- Musquodoboit Harbour
- Ostrea Lake
- Pleasant Point
- Head of Jeddore, West Jeddore, East Jeddore, Jeddore Oyster Pond
- Salmon River Bridge
- Lake Charlotte, Upper Lakeville
- Clam Harbour, Clam Bay
- Little Harbour
- Ship Harbour, Lower Ship Harbour, East Ship Harbour
- Owl's Head
- DeBaie's Cove

Pleasant Point Lighthouse located near the home of the Kent Family. 1999 (AW)

INTRODUCTION

This area, isolated from Halifax and Dartmouth until roads were built, developed slowly. One or two houses were built by fishermen who used boats to reach the different settlements. In time, the government in Halifax recognized the need to encourage settlement further along the coastline, and roads were soon constructed, linking the communities as they developed.

The communities nestled along the coves and inlets in the region of Musquodoboit Harbour were first settled by the descendants of the Foreign Protestants who arrived in Halifax with Governor

Edward Cornwallis in 1749. They were joined in 1784 by a number of United Empire Loyalists in the aftermath of the American Revolution.

WEST PETPESWICK, EAST PETPESWICK

The East and West Petpeswick communities lie on the opposite shores of Petpeswick Harbour, north of Petpeswick Inlet and a little south of Musquodoboit Harbour. The Mi'kmaq called the area "Koolpijwik" meaning "the river eddies in rapids."

On the west side of the harbour, an Acadian family by the name of Greenough (Greno or Grenon) settled in an area referred to as Greenough Settlement around 1768. The family was originally from Port Royal (Annapolis Royal), where Francis Pierre Grenon was born. During the expulsion of the Acadians in 1755, the family escaped to the St. John River area of New Brunswick, later returning to settle in various parts of Halifax County and near Petpeswick Harbour. Today, many still think of the Greenough Settlement—though part of the Petpeswick Harbour settlements—as a separate community.

The Youngs was another Acadian family who settled in the region. Originally spelled LeJeunes, the family name was anglicized after intermarriage with English families in the same settlement. The LaJeunes had arrived in Petpeswick from the Chezzetcook area.

The first land grant of eight thousand acres was handed out to seven pioneer families in 1771. It covered a vast area, from Petpeswick to the Musquodoboit Inlet. Each family was to clear three acres of

Fishing sheds situated on the shore of the Petpeswick Harbour. (NSARM)

land for every fifty they owned, and all within three years. It was a difficult to accomplish, and all but the families of John and George Bayer gave up. In 1779, the Bayer family received full title to their land which became known as Bayer's Point and is still referred to as Bayer's Settlement.

Family tradition states that George Bayer, who was reputed to have a beautiful singing voice, met the Duke of Kent during a visit by the Duke in the 1770s. His land grant was given in payment for a song.

A scenic view of Petpeswick Harbour today. 1999 (AW)

The two Bayer brothers left numerous descendants. The Bayer children in time became landowners in many parts of the Halifax Regional Municipality, including in Halifax with Bayer's Road named for the family.

The Petpeswick settlement grew slowly. By 1827, only seventeen families resided in the area, among them the Anderson, Gilbert, Conrod, and Gaetzes. But as new industry was attracted to the region, the population began to increase.

Similar to many small communities located along the Eastern Shore, Petpeswick enjoyed economic prosperity with the discovery of gold during the latter half of the nineteenth century. Within a very short time period, two hundred local men had been employed by the Petpeswick Gold Mining Company. As the gold petered out, local people turned to other forms of employment. Lumbering sustained many. At the turn of the twentieth century, Omer Gastonquay and George Burrill operated a successful silver fox farm, with their furs being shipped to markets as far away as London, England.

Today's visitors are attracted to the five-kilometer long Martinique Beach Provincial Park (known as the longest sand beach in Nova Scotia), with its white sands and saltwater wild fowl. It is a nesting place for the endangered Piping Plover as well as for the Black Ducks and Canada Geese that winter at a bird sanctuary adjoining the beach.

Musquodoboit Harbour

The community of Musquodoboit Harbour is situated at the mouth of the Musquodoboit River, about thirty-two kilometers east of Dartmouth. The Mi'kmaq called it "Mooskudoboogwek," which means "suddenly widening out after a narrow entrance at the mouth." The village's name is an anglicized version of the Mi'kmaq word.

The Musquodoboit district, encompassing an area from the Harbour

Logs floating in the Musquodoboit Harbour with the Boom Bridge and the Logan family home in the background. (NSARM)

A railway crew constructing the trestle bridge, as part of the railway line officially opened July 1, 1916 from Woodside travelling towards Musquodoboit Harbour. (MRM)

to Chezzetcook, once teemed with wildlife. Moose, bears, and deer roamed the woods while nearby lakes were filled with salmon and trout.

The Musquodoboit Railway Station built between 1916-1918 and reopened as a museum and information center in 1975. (Courtesy of HRM and P.M. Franklin)

A 1909 postcard view of Bayer's Bridge, a wooden covered bridge on the Musquodoboit River just below Rowling's Mill. (MRM)

Settlement of the area followed the usual pattern. In 1771, seven families received land grants, including the family of Michael Brown. These pioneers were joined by Loyalists in the 1780s, among them the MacKay, Taylor, Guild, Jones, Rowling, Stoddard, Bonn, and Stevens families.

Other settlers followed. John Turpel arrived in 1791. Nicholas Goold (Gould), an Englishman from Newfoundland, came in 1810. In 1819, John Anderson and his seven sons arrived from Scotland establishing saw, grist, and oat mills.

Ann Anderson who was the fourth child of John Anderson married Dr. Alexander Wallace. After his death in 1845, his wealthy widow moved home to Musquodoboit Harbour and had Rosebank Cottage built next to her father's home. After Ann's death she willed the beautiful cottage to her brother Charles, who, in turn, bequeathed it to his wife. However, following her death, the property left the Anderson family. The property was restored by Mr. and Mrs. Ralph Morton and is considered to be "one of the gems of the Eastern Shore" and is a provincially registered heritage property.

Among the Foreign Protestant settlers from the Lunenburg area, came George and John Gaetz (Gates) as well as Henry Ritcey, also known as Hen-Ritcie. Descendants of the Gaetz and Ritcey families still live in the community.

Aussie Ritcey, William Gaetz and Charles Ritcey in front of the 'Rolling Rock' near Bayers Mill Road ca. 1927. (MRM)

The Gaetz family established the area known as Gates Settlement. On the north east side of the harbour, Smith Settlement, was settled in the early 1800s by John Smith and his family. They were joined in 1815 by Thomas Crow, another Englishman from Scotland. It was a common practice for travellers in a region to refer to various settlements by the surnames of the families who settled there.

Clairmont Hotel was located near the site of the present RCMP station, taken ca. 1940. The posted signs give the traveller directions to the nearby communities. (HRM)

New businesses soon developed in the community. The Stevens family established a box factory, located on Bayer Lake, producing from three to five hundred boxes a day, as well as a carding mill. Several hotels were constructed and operated by the Chisholm, Gardner, Faulkner and Crawford families. Among those who are listed in the Gardner Hotel register include William Esson, William Anderson, W.S. Fielding, and a number of other prominent travellers.

Today, Musquodoboit Harbour is a self-contained community. The Musquodoboit Railway Museum, operated by the Musquodoboit Heritage Society is a Tourist Information Centre. The Society is dedicated to preserving the history of the families and the settlements located in the area. The museum has a room for genealogists to conduct historical research. Visitors can also view photographs of the area and explore a 1918 Canadian National Railway Station, including the train's engine, flat car and caboose, as well as numerous historical artifacts.

Since sections of the railway tracks throughout the Halifax Regional Municipality are no longer needed, various communities are putting the lines to good use as trailways. The Musquodoboit Trailways Association was recently formed to revitalize the use of the former railway lines. In 1998, this trailway was officially opened and became the first portion of the Trans Canada Trail to open to the public. It extends 17.5 kilometers between Musquodoboit Harbour and Gibralter Rock passing through the woodlands of Route #357.

Ostrea Lake

Ostrea Lake, is named after the Latin word "ostrea" for oysters. It is said that one of the earliest settlers by the name of Staynor planted oysters in a nearby lake, thus giving the community its name, but there is nothing to suggest this is more than legend. The settlement itself is on the shore of Musquodoboit Harbour.

Captain and Mrs. Martin Williams in Ostrea Lake during the 1950s. (NSARM)

The community, situated forty kilometers southeast of Dartmouth, was settled by the descendants of some of the German Protestants who accompanied Cornwallis to Halifax. In 1786, Matthew Lexon and John Turpel, both of German ancestry, received the first land grants. In

1808, Patrick Williams arrived with his family. The Williams, an Irish family from Newfoundland, had first settled among the Acadians near Chezzetcook, married into a Protestant family and subsequently moved to Ostrea Lake. For awhile the area was known as Williams Settlement. Other German settlers, including the Bowser family, arrived during the 1830s. The settlers either fished or were involved in small-scale farming. In time, the community established a post office and erected an Anglican Church.

A cemetery has been uncovered on a small island in the harbour across from Ostrea Lake. The island was granted to Mi'kmaq chief Francis Nose (Knowles). Many of the former residents of Ostrea Lake, Point Pleasant, and the Jeddore communities, as well as Mi'kmaq families, are interred in this cemetery.

Pleasant Point

Pleasant Point, on the east side of Musquodoboit Harbour was originally known as Kent Island and is still referred to by that name. William Kent, an Englishman who had served in the Royal Navy for fifteen years, was discharged in 1813. He was offered the post of Warden at the Melville Prison on Halifax's North West Arm. In 1818 the family received a land grant and became the first settlers to reside on the island. It could only be reached by boat until a bridge was built connecting the island to the mainland across Oyster Pond Run.

Other families continued to move to the island. In 1840, John Jacob Nauffts, who had been born in Halifax, the son of a German Hessian soldier, arrived at the settlement. The Slaunwhite family arrived during the mid-1850s. Frederick Slaunwhite was the direct descendant of a German family who had received a land grant in the Lunenburg area one hundred years earlier. He and his wife Sophia (Baker) of Tancook Island, Lunenburg County, had eight children. Today descendants of these various families can be found residing in the Pleasant Point area.

At the end of Kent Road stands the Pleasant Point Lighthouse. Though no longer is use, it is one of seven lighthouses still standing on the Eastern Shore. Ivan Kent, present owner of the lighthouse is the third generation of his family to have kept the light at the Point. Oral tradition states that Admiral Nelson haunts the lighthouse since Mr. Kent's ancestor sailed with the famous admiral.

Head of Jeddore, West Jeddore, East Jeddore, Jeddore Oyster Pond

The four Jeddore communities extend around the horseshoe-shaped Jeddore Harbour, with Jeddore Oyster Pond (known locally as simply Oyster Pond) separated from the others by the community of Salmon River Bridge. To the Mi'kmaq, the pond was known as "Pajedoobaachk" meaning "wave washed" or the more descriptive "buried by the rolling wave." To local residents it became Oyster Pond for the oysters supposedly found in the area.

Jeddore Rock Island with the fishermen hoisting their fish on to the wharf with the lighthouse in the background. (NSARM)

The French explorer Nicholas Denys arriving in the area in 1672, referred to it as "River of Theodore." In time, this was anglicized to Jeddore. The Right Honorable Earl of Egmont received a land grant in the area and began advertising for settlers as early as 1769. However, it was not until the Loyalists arrived in the 1780s that the population began to increase. They were joined by descendants of a number of the Foreign Protestants from Lunenburg County.

Many of the families who settled in the Jeddore region still have descendants living there. Some of the earliest Loyalists included Edward Hare, who received a grant in 1786 for land on the east side of Lake Egmont. Blacksmith Joseph Baker and fellow Loyalist John Day arrived the same year. Fifteen years later they were joined by Benjamin Arnold, a Loyalist from Rhode Island or Connecticut, who had first settled in Liverpool, Queens County. Joseph Dooks (Dukes), a resident of Armdale, a suburb of Halifax, arrived at Jeddore Harbour in 1801, as did John Doyle, an Irishman born in Nova Scotia who made barrels for packing salted fish.

John Henry Myers, the son of a Loyalist by the name of Andrew Myers received a grant in 1812. He settled his family to the east of Jeddore Harbour. His father received the piece of land that juts out into the harbour known as Myer's Point. The family was self-sufficient, raising their own food, and fishing to supplement their income. Today the Myers family home is the Fisherman's Life Museum, which opened in 1973. Interpreters explain how the Myers family with thirteen daughters lived in this small fisherman's house believed to have been built around 1857.

The Mitchell family also settled near Myer's Point. Colin Mitchell, just sixteen-years-old when his parents brought him from Scotland, became an apprentice to a large landowner on the Eastern Shore by the name of Sir Colin Campbell. Sir Colin sold some of his land to John George Webber and young Colin Mitchell eventually married Catherine Webber and purchased land in Oyster Pond around 1813. Members of the Mitchell family were keepers of the Jeddore Rock Lighthouse for more than forty years.

A scenic view of East Jeddore, 1999 (AW)

Issac Hopkins, whose family came to America on the Mayflower, was born in Barrington, Shelburne County, and arrived in Jeddore in the 1820s. Other settlers were of German descent. Bernard Faulkner (Volcher) arrived with his parents as Foreign Protestants and moved to Jeddore around 1830. The Harpell family from Germany became community leaders. Henry

A scenic view of the West Jeddore area. 1999 (AW)

Jennex (Shenick) was a German Hessian soldier who arrived around 1838. The Hartlin (Hartlen) brothers, George and Colin, also descendants of Foreign Protestants, moved to what became known as Hartlin Settlement.

There is a war memorial surrounded by a small park in Jeddore Oyster Pond to commemorate those who served in the First and Second World Wars. The monument was first built in 1926 at the crossroads of Highway #7 and East Jeddore Road, then moved to its new location when the new highway was built. Among the families who lost sons and daughters during the Great War were the Webbers, Mitchells, Stoddards, and Myers. A plaque was added after the Second World War in memory of those who died during that war, including members of the Baker, Bowser, Day, Faulkner, Guild, Hartling, Jennex, and Mitchell families.

The Meyer family's home now the Fisherman's Life Museum in Jeddore Oyster Pond. 1999 (HRM)

Salmon River Bridge

Located at the head of Jeddore Harbour, this small community is situated beside the bridge over the Salmon River. The river is named for the salmon that migrate up to spawn each year. The first bridge erected over the river was built in February 1853 with a second one replacing it in 1883.

The Mi'kmaq, who camped along the river during summer months, called this area "Wineboogwechk," which translates oddly as "a crooked, ugly, flowing river."

Loyalist veterans of the American Revolution were among the first to settle in the community; among them Hugh Dunnegan who received the first land grant and Corporal Joseph Langley who received the second, both in 1786.

Mr. Day of Salmon River Bridge. (NSARM)

For awhile, the Salmon River settlement flourished after Peter Paul, a Mi'kmaq, discovered gold in August 1880 with lead discovered a few weeks later. But as the minerals were depleted the economic boom came to an end and the community returned to fishing as a way of life

LAKE CHARLOTTE/UPPER LAKEVILLE

Lake Charlotte was named in honour of Princess Charlotte, Augusta of Wales, who died in 1817 shortly after the area was settled. Approximately fifty kilometers south east of Dartmouth, the settlement was once a part of the Sheet Harbour district but boundary changes established it as a community. At one time it was also a part of a chain of lakes, with the communities known as Upper and Lower Lakeville on opposite ends of the lake. This was too confusing for the postal service, so in 1864, Lower Lakeville was renamed Ship Harbour Lake for a short period of time, eventually being changed to Lake Charlotte.

Among the first to arrive at Lake Charlotte were several Loyalist families, including four Webber brothers, the sons of John George Webber of nearby Clam Harbour. John Webber and his wife Elizabeth Doull had arrived with four hundred families to settle in Nova Scotia. Their ship, however, landed in South Carolina where they settled until the American Revolution drove them north in 1785. Upper Lakeville was settled by the families of George and Andrew Siteman (Sideman) in 1814, and Patrick O'Bryan (O'Brian) an Irishman in 1815.

By 1904, there was a population of 160, one hotel, and a general store. Work was found in the lumbering industry since logs could be floated across the lake in summer months and hauled out of the woods by horse and sleigh in the winter. In 1937, by an Act of Legislature the name of Ship Harbour Lake was officially changed to Lake Charlotte.

A photograph of Lake Charlotte, formerly known as Ship Harbour Lake with the waterfall over Mill Brook, taken ca. 1927. (NSARM)

Storefronts in Lake Charlotte, 1999 (AW)

Clam Harbour

The Mi'kmaq referred to the Clam Harbour area as "Asegadich" meaning "clam gathering place." The first residents called it Clam Cove. It became Clam Harbour after the cove was dredged making it easier for boats to sail into the harbour. Clams are plentiful along the shores of the sandy beach and residents can be seen digging for them at low tide.

Mr. Stoddart, a descendant of one of the founding families. (NSARM)

Sir Colin Campbell of Scotland, along with members of his family, was the first to settle in Clam Harbour around 1765. Together with Robert Campbell Sr. and Jr. and Duncan Campbell, the family received over 2,000 acres. Sir Colin, a retired major in the army, moved to Jeddore but the rest of his extended family remained in the vicinity of Clam Harbour.

The Webber brothers of Lake Charlotte, along with their brother-in-law Colin Mitchell, purchased some of the Campbell lands, as did Thomas Stoddard who acquired ownership of land on the west side of Clam Harbour as well as Clam Harbour Beach in 1799. The Stoddard family to this day tells the story of Sir Colin Campbell's pistol. Apparently a member of the Stoddard family was farming his land when he stumbled upon a pistol buried in the ground. It was a flintlock with a silver plate on the stock,

A beautiful example of the Clam Harbour Beach sandcastle sculpture competition, held annually in August. (Courtesy of HRM and P. M. Franklin)

engraved with the words "Colin Campbell, Smithy Green." Other settlers have found arrowheads and French musket balls embedded in the ground.

The Webber family were said to have landed on a point of land near Clam Bay and were so weary that they pitched their tents where they stood and fell asleep. Apparently they slept so long that they decided to name the area "Sleepy Head Point," a name that can be found on the 1864 Ambrose Church map of Halifax County.

Clam Harbour Beach is one of HRM's more popular recreational summer places. 1999 (AW)

Other families also arrived, many of them related to settlers in nearby communities. John Russell and John Robson arrived with their families in 1826 and each settled a 200-acre grant. John Robson, a fisherman, married Susanna Siteman in 1828 and had nine children. They were joined by the Stevens and Hutt families from Nova Scotia's South Shore. Many of the descendants of these families still reside in the area. Today Clam Harbour Beach is known as a popular tourist attraction—especially for its annual sand sculpture competition held in August.

LITTLE HARBOUR

A few kilometers from Clam Harbour is the community of Little Harbour. The Mi'kmaq named it "Seegunakigunuk," meaning "torn in shreds or sail scraps."

A scenic view of the small fishing community of Little Harbour. 1999 (AW)

Members of the Stoddard family purchased land from Sir Colin Campbell in 1799 which included the Little Harbour area. The family were Loyalists who arrived in the mid-1780s. They also lived in many parts of Nova Scotia including, for a while, Point Pleasant Park situated at the entrance to Halifax Harbour. Family tradition suggests the family moved because soldiers stationed nearby often pilfered their livestock and personal belongings.

Other families still living in the Little Harbour area include those with the surnames Weaver, Newcomb, and Tucker, who arrived in the 1820s as fishermen.

SHIP HARBOUR

To the Mi'kmaq this area was called "Tedumunaboogwek" which means "a water-worn rock." According to oral tradition, the present name came from the shape of the cliffs at the head of Ship Harbour that is said to resemble a ship in full sail. The community has also been known as Knowles Harbour after a settler of that name, as well as Colville Harbour after Alex and Charles Colville who were granted land in 1766.

Three communities along the Eastern Shore share the name of Ship Harbour, with Lower and East Ship Harbour situated on opposite shores of the harbour.

Among the earliest settlers were Loyalists from South Carolina who arrived aboard the ship *Argo*. They included James Goff, George Weaver, Adam Negeson, Andrew Myers, Nicholas Crum (Crumb), Christian Long, Lawrence Marks, Conrad Shady, John Melon, Chambers Blakeley, and Henry Siteman. Many of these families moved to areas near Ship Harbour, creating new settlements.

The homestead of George Siteman of Lower Ship Harbour built around 1854. (NSARM)

The Loyalist settlers consisted of families of different ethnic backgrounds but were united in their decision to live in a country loyal to the British crown. Chambers Blakeley was Irish while John Lawrence Marks, George Weaver, Andrew Miles and Henry Siteman were German. Joseph Lumb (or Lamb) was an English sailor who had settled in Virginia in 1775, had been drafted into the militia and then had moved to Ship Harbour after the American Revolution. Archibald Gilchrist, of Scottish origin, had been discharged from the British navy in New Brunswick and moved to Ship Harbour in 1822. John Monk, born in Herring Cove, moved to Ship Harbour, married three times and had a total of ten children. Some of their descendants still live in and around the community.

A portrait photograph of Charles A. Siteman, son of George and Jane (Newcomb) Siteman, descendants of the original founding families of the Ship Harbour area. (NSARM)

Ship Harbour Road prior to being developed into a paved two lane highway. (NSARM)

Fishing, supplemented by a little family farming, has sustained the families through the years. Today the harbour is dotted with numerous small buoys that mark the site of a cultivated mussel farm, a newly established and prosperous fishing enterprise.

Present-day Ship Harbour 1999 (AW)

Owl's Head Harbour

The Mi'kmaq called the Owl's Head Harbour area "Phyropskook" or "Pujooopskook" which is said to mean "cormorant rock," after the wild fowl that can be seen along the Nova Scotian coastline. To settlers who came to this part of the coast some sixty kilometers from Dartmouth, the rock formation at the entrance resembled an owl perched on a rock in the harbour. So the community became Owl's Head Bay and Owl's Head Harbour. A map of Nova Scotia, charted by Desbarres, named the area Kepple Harbour after Admiral Augustus Kepple of the British Navy. But as with many other regions named by Desbarres, it changed once settlers arrived.

By 1784, thirty land grants had been issued. However by 1817, the population had dwindled to ten families. Some of the original settlers had been disbanded soldiers who were granted land situated on the east side of the harbour. David Palmer, an early settler, had been apprentice to his Uncle Richard Palmer of Manchester, England who had trained in the art of "ironmongering." David travelled to the United States and after the War of 1812, arrived in Nova Scotia receiving a grant at Owl's Head Harbour. In 1819 Palmer married Catherine Parker. She was the daughter of Alex Fraser of Sheet Harbour, the widow of Phineas Parker and already had six children. Although still a rural area, some of the descendants of the first settlers still reside at Owl's Head Harbour.

DeBaie's Cove (DeBay Cove)

Approximately thirty-five kilometers south west of Sheet Harbour lies the community of DeBaie's Cove. The name of the community may have originated from the name of a family that settled here before the Loyalists arrived.

The community was once part of a large land grant issued to thirty Loyalist families in 1784. Edward Day, an Irishman, was one of the first to receive a grant that included this settlement and the area first became known as Day's Cove. It may be that Day's Cove, through a series of mispronunciations over the years, was changed to (DeBay Cove) Debaie's Cove.

Norman Hutt Boatbuilders, a family business in the Owl's Head Harbour area. 1999 (AW)

Others who followed

Edward Day included such Loyalist families as Goff, Mark, Crum, Weaver, Shady, Sideman (Siteman), Newgeser (Negeson), Song, Blakeley, and Melton.

For years, shipbuilding has sustained the community and surrounding areas. Today DeBaie's Cove (DeBay Cove) is recognized for the expert craftsmanship of the pleasure craft and cruising boats being constructed in the community.

A small home designed to look like a lighthouse overlooking Debaie's Cove. 1999 (AW)

Chapter Five

MOOSELAND TO LISCOMB SANCTUARY

- Mooseland
- Marinette
- Murphy's Cove
- Pleasant Harbour
- Tangier
- Pope's Harbour
- Spry Harbour, Spry Bay
- Taylor Head
- Mushaboom
- Sheet Harbour, Sheet Harbour Passage, Sober Island
- Watt Section
- Beaver Harbour
- Lewiston
- Port Dufferin
- West Newdy Quoddy and East Quoddy
- Harrigan Cove
- Moosehead
- Necum Teuch
- Mitchell Bay
- Ecum Secum
- Moser River
- Lochaber Mines
- Malay Falls
- Liscomb Sanctuary

A view of the lighthouse on Sheet Harbour Rock Island situated in Sheet Harbour. (NSARM)

INTRODUCTION

Most communities along the Eastern Shore were settled by Loyalists and descendants of Foreign Protestants who arrived around 1783 following the American Revolution. A few had already lived in other parts of Nova Scotia and were attracted to the heavily forested region of Sheet Harbour. These settlers knew well the hardships involved in clearing land for homes and farms, but they found the soil fertile and many subsidized their large families with produce from vegetable gardens.

Those who settled along the coast tended to be fishermen or ship builders. The ships were needed to transport lumber and supply other necessities not available to the settlers in their new land. During early settlement the communities of Beaver Harbour, Port Dufferin, and Quoddy were known as Beaver Harbour and the area from Quoddy to Ecum Secum was referred to as the "Bay of Islands."

As communities developed, land along the coast became scarce and families began to move inland. Periodically, the government would improve the roads so that residents could get their produce to the coast for shipment or to sell in local markets. Several settlements, such as Tangier and Mooseland, enjoyed a brief economic boom after the discovery of gold in the mid-1800s.

Today, people continue to be attracted to this region with its paved roads, unspoiled beauty and easy access to the Eastern Shore. It has become a favourite vacation spot for tourists.

MOOSELAND

Mooseland, named for the moose that once abounded in the forests, is better known for its gold. The first discovery was made in 1857 by Lieutenant C. L'Estrange, who came across quartz containing gold while out moose hunting. He did not explore further; however, in 1861, John Gerrish Pulsifer, a farmer from Musquodoboit, searched the same area and came across a quartz boulder containing gold. Nova Scotia's first gold rush was on!

News of the discovery spread far and wide, and soon gold was found in other parts of the Eastern Shore. A second gold rush took place in 1896 and reached its peak in 1898. Alfred Nobel's invention of dynamite meant that blasting rocks could speed up the mining process. Soon gold was being discovered in other parts of Canada and the miners and their families moved on, causing a decline in gold production. A third gold rush in the 1920s was sparked by a demand for arsenopyrite, a mineral contained in Nova Scotia's gold deposits. The search was on for more deposits and continued for nearly ten years. By the mid to late 1930s, the gold rush had petered out, the miners had gone and Mooseland had become a ghost town.

Gold may have been the village's main commodity, but new businesses were slowly established. In 1862, Francis Ellerhauser constructed the first stamp mill. As settlers arrived such as James Hilchie in 1865, the Leslie family in 1872, and the Prests in 1884 the lumber business became established and sawmills were erected. While poor management and incompetence lead to a decline in the gold production, lumbering continued as a way of life. There was even an attempt in 1897 to change the name of the settlement by an Act of Legislation from Mooseland to Arlington, but the new name never caught on.

Over the past fifty years, new homes were built in the Mooseland area. New road construction meant that residents who preferred living in the country could easily reach the coastal communities for shopping and other amenities.

Marinette

Marinette is located about ten kilometers upstream on Sheet Harbour River. The name of the area may have had a connection with a firm in Wisconsin known as the Marinette Company, but no one knows for sure. One of the first families to settle in Marinette was that of David Redmond, an Irishman from Country Antrim, Ireland. He originally settled in the Musquodoboit area but in 1828 he petitioned for another land grant. Together with Edward Rutledge and Thomas Pendergast, Mr. Redmond helped to establish the Marinette community.

Murphy's Cove

At the head of Shoal Bay lies Murphy's Cove, named for the Murphy family from Ireland. Thomas Murphy and his wife Elizabeth of Tangier were the first settlers. They had eight children according to the 1827 census. Others who joined the Murphys included John Beaver, George Shellnut, Sr. and Jr., and Allen Cameron, as well as the Edwards, Hilchie, Newcombe and Butler families.

A scenic view of present day Murphy's Cove. 1999 (AW)

Pleasant Harbour

The first settlers to reside in Pleasant Harbour referred to the area as Saunders Harbour. Later it was called Tangier-Shoal Bay but by an Act of Legislature it was changed to its present name in 1866.

The first family to settle at the head of Shoal Bay were the Newcombe family. This family was originally from the New England States and was part of a group from Lebanon, Connecticut, who first settled in Kings County. In 1761, three Newcombe brothers arrived in Pleasant Harbour. In 1784, they were joined by one of their sons, Oliver Newcombe, who had been living at Ship Harbour under the Captain Thomas Green's grant. Others who arrived in Pleasant Harbour included the Glawson and Lynch families.

Mr. A. J. Moore of Pleasant Harbour. (NSARM)

A scenic view of present-day Pleasant Harbour. 1999 (AW)

TANGIER

At the head of Tangier Harbour, about twenty kilometers southwest of Sheet Harbour lies the community of Tangier. To the Mi'kmaq, it was "Wospegeak," meaning "the sunshine is reflected from the water." It is not known how it got its present name. Some say it may have been derived from the name of a ship that was wrecked off shore in 1830. Others believe it may be connected to the Moroccan seaport of Tangier. Portugal governed Morocco during the time when Portuguese fishermen often sailed to Nova Scotia to fish.

A general view of the bridge over the Tangier River. 1999 (AW)

The first land grant was issued to the Loyalist family of Philip, John, and Thomas Newton in 1785. By 1790 the Moxon and Sullivan families had joined them. In 1827 a number of families descended from the Foreign Protestants of Lunenburg County arrived, including those by the names of Jennings, Hutt, Myersom, Mason, Welsh, and Lawlor.

Peter Mason, one of the Foreign Protestant descendants, discovered gold in 1861. That discovery led to approximately thirty years of gold mining in the Tangier region and many miners became quite prosperous. Lumbering took over as the gold disappeared. Prospecting for gold, however, still continues to this day on a small scale.

POPE'S HARBOUR

The Mi'kmaq called the area to the east of Tangier, "Kwemoodech," "little loon place," or "Kwemoodeech." (The extra "e" changes the meaning to "a small harbour.") It was once referred to as Dean Harbour and may have been changed to Pope's Harbour after the name of an early settler.

The first land grant went to Lieutenant Samuel Harris who received two thousand acres in 1773. A second warrant to survey 250 acres by Patrick Weirgon was issued in 1786. But it was the settlers who arrived during the early 1800s, many of them the sons and daughters of Foreign Protestants, whose descendants still remain in the area today.

David Hilchey (Ueltschi) was from Switzerland and arrived in Nova Scotia as a child. He married Sophie West and the couple had ten children. Abraham Bollong, from Germany, lived to be a very old man in the community. Robert Henry of Ireland was a violinist who made his own instruments and composed music. He arrived in Nova Scotia in 1854 and married Catherine Edwards.

Lobster traps waiting to be loaded on the fishing boats near Pope's Harbour. 1999 (AW)

Spry Harbour, Spry Bay

The Mi'kmaq called the Spry Bay area "Sebimkooaak," meaning "a bog extending across." Spry may have been an early settler, or the small community may have been named in honour of Colonel William Spry. Colonel Spry was the Chief Engineer who was stationed in Halifax in the 1770s and was responsible for the daily operations of the fortifications surrounding the city. The community has had other names over the years. A survey map in 1896 identifies it as Leslies Harbour and Henleys Harbour after two settlers. The area has also been known as Taylors Bay, and some early maps have it recorded as Winchelsea Harbour, named for a port in Sussex, England.

Overlooking Spry Harbour on a sunny afternoon. 1999 (AW)

The first land grant went to Samuel Harris who received two thousand acres in 1773. Among the settlers was Emanuel Josey (Jewezey) who was born in Portugal and shipwrecked at the entrance to Sheet Harbour. Thankful to reach dry land, he decided to stay in nearby Spry Bay. The 1827 census lists him as E. Jewez, a fisherman with eleven children. Another early settler was Thomas Walsh, an Irishman and farmer born in Nova Scotia. He had five children. Many of the residents of Spry Harbour and Spry Bay are descendants of these original families, while a number of Dutch families settled on the north side of Spry Bay in a place known as Dutch Town.

Today, just to the east of Spry Harbour is Spry Bay Provincial Park, a lovely rest stop for travellers.

Taylor Head

Situated between Spry Bay and Mushaboom Harbour is the community of Taylor Head. The area was most likely named for an early settler though DesBarres called it Cape Spry.

The first family—according to popular wisdom—to land at Taylor Head was the McCarthys who arrived in the 1780s from Ireland via Holland and the United States. Mrs. McCarthy, a widow, and her two Loyalist sons arrived from South Carolina shortly after the American Revolution ended. She married a settler from Ship Harbour and some members of her family married into the Siteman family. By 1814, George McCarthy shared a land grant with the Eisan family but six years later he moved to McCarthy's Hill at Mushaboom. However, the 1827 census lists him residing at Taylor Head once more.

In 1818, the community was referred to as Cape Taylor Head, but by 1829 the area was once again known as Cape Spry. By 1838 many of the settlers farmed at Taylor's Head, among them George McCarthy Sr. and Jr., as well as John, Archibald, Benjamin and Owen Newcomb.

Taylor's Head Provincial Park at Taylor Head has picnic areas and boardwalks to the beach. There are also hiking trails that extend along Mushaboom Harbour to the end of the peninsula. Gerrard Island, within the Taylor's Head area, is named after the Gerrard family. Henry Gerrard of England was living there in 1827, though he later moved to

Popes Harbour. John Gerrard, also living on the island in 1827, married Mary Glawson and many of his ancestors are buried on the island.

MUSHABOOM

The community of Mushaboom is located about ten kilometers southwest of Sheet Harbour. The place received its name from an English version of the Mi'kmaq word "Moosaboon-elagwaak," meaning "a pile of hair." Legend has it that fairies used to play ball there, running and seizing each other's hair, pulling some out and tossing it on the ground. It is certainly a more imaginative name than Winchester Harbour which it had been previously named in honour of one of the transport ships that brought settlers to Nova Scotia in 1749.

A scenic view of Mushaboom Harbour. 1999 (AW)

First to settle in the area was George Fred Boutilier of Lunenburg County, who arrived with his wife Margaret Dauphinee in 1821. Both traced their origins to Foreign Protestants. The Boutiliers and their children settled on Boutilier's Island in the bay and many of the Boutilier descendants still live in the area.

SHEET HARBOUR

The village of Sheet Harbour is over one hundred kilometers east of Dartmouth. This harbour was once known to the Mi'kmaq as "Weijooik," which means "flowing wildly or running crazily." By the 1770s, the region was called Campbell Town though no one of that name is known to have settled here. The name may have referred to one of the officers involved in the settlement of Nova Scotia, Lord William

Campbell. He was Captain-General and Governor-in-Chief of the colony from 1766 to 1773.

When Simon Rutledge, a Northern Ireland soldier, arrived in the area there were still Mi'kmaq camping on the land granted to the Rutledge family. He is said to have been the first white man to settle in this region. Land grants were issued between 1773 and 1784, mostly to veterans or refugees of the American Revolution. When the settlers arrived, they found that the forests extended down to the coastline. Some of the disbanded soldiers left once their rations were gone: they were not able to cope as farmers.

Havelock M. Hart's lumber mill on Sheet Harbour's West River in1880, later purchased by Rhodes and Curry in 1902. (NSARM)

The settlers to first arrive chose the east side of the harbour to build their homin a place called Watts Section. Members of the Rutledges were joined by the Fraser, Greer, and Curry families as well as several others. The land grant was divided into fifty-nine lots.

In 1773, Alexander Fraser arrived at Pictou aboard the Hector, one of the first of a number of Scottish immigrants to settle in Sheet Harbour. He left to join the army in Halifax and for a while fought in the American Revolution. On being discharged, he returned to Nova Scotia, received a land grant and married Alice MacGregor. He and his four sons—Alex, John, James, and Simon—set up the very successful Fraser's Shipyards.

Around the same time in 1787, Englishman John Augusta Behie arrived from Virginia, settled on a grant known as Behiefields and married Ann Balcom of Salmon River. Many of his descendants still reside in and around Sheet Harbour.

By 1807, the area was known as Port North and even Manchester for a short while. A few years later, in 1812, William Hall from Devon, England arrived and married Sarah Currie after receiving a part of the Greer grant. Within three years, the Hall family had set up a thriving shipbuilding and lumbering business.

By 1818, the name Sheet Harbour was used in reference to the community. The name is said to have arisen from how the land presents itself from the water—a large white rock resembles a sheet laid out to dry.

The forestry industry has played a major role in the development of Sheet Harbour. By 1850, James Cruickshanks, a direct descendant of Peter Cruickshanks, another Scottish immigrant, began logging operations. Families with names such as Cameron, Dimock, Gallagher, Hogan, Holman, O'Leary, and Pace arrived to work in the sawmills or the forests. More families arrived such as the Low, Kenney, Logan, MacPhee, and MacDonalds.

Sawmills produced the wood that framed the settlers' homes. One of the first mills was built by Thomas Lydiard, a representative of John Greer. By 1884, there was a pulp mill constructed by S.M. Brookfield, William Chisholm, and William MacNab as the chief shareholders.

In the late 1800s, Eric Curry, son of Senator Curry of Amherst, was established as the General Manager of the Sheet Harbour Lumbering Company. The mill exported wood to England and the United States, though some found its way to local markets. The mill, known as Chisholm Mill, was bought by Eric Curry eventually and he, in turn, joined forces with Nelson Rhodes in 1896.

Wood from the Chisholm Mill (and a second portable mill) cut logs that were floated down the West River to the pulp mill. It was renamed West River Mill after being purchased from Havelock Hart in 1902. William Chisholm was instrumental in establishing Canada's first sulphite pulp mill in 1885, on the East River called the Halifax Wood Fiber Company. Unfortunately, the success of this mill only lasted until 1891, but remnants of this pulp mill site is still visible today.

In time, a hydroelectric plant was constructed to harness the water-energy of the East River and to develop power at Malay Falls to light towns within the Pictou and Eastern Halifax Counties. A dam was placed at the Falls, eight kilometers up the East River from tidal waters.

A storage dam was then built at Mulgrave Lake on the south west branch of the river, about six kilometers from the proposed power plant.

In the 1980s, the economic benefits and opportunities available from Sheet Harbour's naturally deep harbour were finally recognized. With funding provided by the Canada-Nova Scotia Offshore Development Agreement, the Sheet Harbour Marine Industrial Park and Port was completed in 1987. With a 150 meter berthing wharf connected to a large cement pad, the deep-water facility is accessible by road from the Halifax International Airport and the city of Halifax.

About fourteen kilometers from Sheet Harbour on Sheet Harbour Rock is a lighthouse standing defenseless in the wind. Two large rivers,

A present view of the Sheet Harbour's West River taken from the bridge. 1999 (AW)

the East and West Rivers, approach the harbour from opposite directions and flow into it at the same point. At Church Point, where the two rivers join the harbour one is said to be standing where the three bodies of water meet.

Sober Island, located at the eastern entrance to Sheet Harbour Passage got its name, according to oral tradition, from a comment made by the local minister, a Dr. Sprott. After visiting fishermen on the island, he commented that "the island was sober," thus the origin of the island's name.

Before Dr. Sprott's pronouncement, the island was known simply as Sheet Harbour Island and earlier as White Island, after one of the earlier settlers. Just over four kilometers in length and half a kilometer wide, the island is shaped like a pear. It has a fresh water lake and gravel beach, and a small community with its own school and churches.

The causeway that connects Sober Island to the mainland. 1999 (AW)

In 1816, John Moser and John Allen were each given a licence to occupy a quarter of the island to begin fishing operations. Then, in 1883, C.P. Matlacks of Portland, Maine, opened a lobster factory that employed a number of people from nearby communities.

In the late 1880s, land grants were given to Henry Balcom (fifty acres) and John Verge (thirty acres). Howard Verge operated a very successful fish company, J.D. Verge and Sons, which also was a fish buying and curing establishment.

In 1919, small grants were issued to Martin Harnish and Howard Verge. A year later Andrew Markie and Hedley Munro each received about sixty acres. But fishing has always remained an important way of life on the island.

Watt Section

Watt Section, along the east side of Sheet Harbour, is named for William Watt. Born in Devonshire, England, though of Scottish ancestry, he had been in the British navy for seven years before he decided to jump ship in Halifax. From there he went to Barrington Passage where he met his wife. Then, in 1815, the Watt family and other settlers from the Shelburne region, moved to Watt Section, though it was not until 1844 that the community received its official name. By that time, William Watt had a reputation as one of the largest landowners in the area.

While Watt may have the distinction of having the settlement named for him, he was not the first settler. The area was part of a land grant issued to Jonathan Belcher in 1773, then the Chief Justice of Nova Scotia. It took ten years for settlement to begin but by 1783 both John Low and Simon Rutledge had built homes here, though at the time it was considered to be a part of Sheet Harbour.

Near the water at Watt Section is an old cemetery containing the graves of many early settlers, including those with the names of Lowe, Rutledge, Jollymore, LeBlanc, Smith, Martin, McCarthy, Helpard, and Verge. In those days, graveyards abutted the water's edge because funeral processions travelled by boat.

A view of the new container pier situated on the opposite shore of the small community of Watt's Section. 1999 (AW)

BEAVER HARBOUR

"Kobetawakwemoode" is the Mi'kmaq name for the Beaver Harbour area. Indian folklore says that Glooscap, a Mi'kmaq folk-hero, threw a large rock at a mystical beaver in the harbour. On an Acadian map of 1703, it is recorded as "Havre au Castor" or "Beaver Harbour." Originally Beaver Harbour included Port Dufferin and Quoddy within its boundaries.

Land grants in the area were first issued to Halifax merchant John Lawson in 1787. At the same time a number of Loyalist families were arriving in the community. One group, on its way to take up land claims in the Antigonish region, was forced to winter over in Beaver Harbour when ice encased their ship. Rather than move on in the spring they petitioned for grants to stay in the region.

Many descendants of the original settlers remain. The Spears family is descended from William Spears, a Loyalist whose ancestors first settled in Roseway, Shelburne County, in 1819. The family left for Guysborough County, moved on to Back Cove and finally arrived in

Beaver Harbour. By 1834, five families resided in the area.

Other settlers also came, some descendants of Foreign Protestants with such family names as Atkin, Baker, Barkhouse, Hartling, Romkey, Smith, Whitman, Kerr, Owen, Happold, Spears, Dahr, and Harvey. The Hartling family originally spelled their name as Hirtle and both versions of the name can be found in the community and surrounding villages today.

A sand dune extending across Beaver Harbour. 1999 (AW)

LEWISTON

Lewiston, on the north west side of Salmon River Big Lake, is named for the Lewis family of Truro who moved to Lewiston at the end of the 1800s. George and John Lewis and their sons obtained a number of grants in 1892, 1898, and 1899 to establish lumbering operations, such as a hardwood manufacturing plant.

For a time, Lewis and Company operated a clothes' peg factory. Pins were made from hardwood trees—beech, maple, or birch. The system was very clever. Logs were hauled by automatic chain and sent to the "cut off" or sawed into one-meter lengths. From there the logs moved to a rotary saw and were cut into thin strips. A drum cut the strips into lengths of between two and three centimeters. Special blades then trimmed the pins and a slotter machine cut slots into each one. The pins were then sent to a dryer and polisher where they were mixed in soapstone and wax added a finishing touch. Then finally they were boxed at 720 to a set. The factory produced its own boxes as well and over 200 people were employed.

PORT DUFFERIN

Port Dufferin, to the east of Sheet Harbour, was known to the Mi'kmaq as "Pulamooa seboo" (Salmon River). It was officially changed to Port

Dufferin by an Act of Legislation in 1899 to honour the Marquis of Dufferin, Frederick Temple Blackwood, Governor General of Canada from 1872 to 1878.

The first land grant of ten thousand acres, was issued to Colonel John Hale who never set eyes on his land. This was quite a common practice among prominent families who looked on these grants as investments. He did try to persuade Yorkshire families to settle on his grant but they preferred to reside in the Colchester County area.

A portrait photograph of James McLeod (1823-1915) of Port Dufferin. (courtesy of Phillip Hartling)

One of the earliest residents of Port Dufferin was Hector MacLeod (McLeod), a plasterer by trade. Although born in Scotland in 1793, he had lived in Halifax before settling in Port Dufferin, marrying and raising a large family. His son James, a sailor, also had a large family of nine children. Today many MacLeod descendants live in and around Port Dufferin.

A number of other families arrived over the years. Irishman John Casey and his six children settled first in Petpeswick, then at Port Dufferin. Thomas Diggins of Halifax, who was involved in the fishing industry, moved to Port Dufferin and raised five children with his wife Catherine Conrad. John Whitman of Lunenburg County, a relative of the Whitmans of Beaver Harbour, arrived in Port Dufferin in 1809. He helped to build fishing schooners and did some farming on the side to help feed his wife and ten children.

Jacob Barkhouse (Berghaus), born in Gold River, Lunenburg County was a descendant of Foreign Protestant parents. By 1819, Jacob and

Hector Hartling (1872-1937) and Carrie (née Erskine) Hartling of Port Dufferin. (courtesy of Phillip Hartling)

his family were living in Port Dufferin and involved in agriculture. The many Barkhouse descendants found throughout the province of Nova Scotia today are descended from one of Jacob's nine children. Henry Baldwin and John Henry Burgoyne arrived to the area from Sober Island and were originally from St. Margaret's Bay.

The Hartling family homestead located in Port Dufferin, formerly West Port Dufferin, is known as the "Stone House." It was built in 1874 and restored by its present owner, Phillip Hartling. (courtesy of Phillip Hartling)

WEST NEWDY QUODDY AND EAST QUODDY

The two Quoddy communities were once a part of the Beaver Harbour district. The name Newdy Quoddy is an anglicized version of the original Mi'kmaq "Nookakwode" meaning "seal hunting place." Locals refer to the communities as Quoddy.

Among the first families to arrive were Alex and Simon Fraser, descendants of the first Alexander Fraser. Philip and Ann Hartling, the first of the Hartlings to leave Lunenburg County, arrived in Quoddy in 1810 with their twelve children. George Harvey Sr. moved his family around 1819 to this area from Lunenburg. His son George Jr., played a major role in the ship building industry.

Others included the Bezansons, descendants of Foreign Protestants, who arrived in 1821 on the escheated lands of Colonel John Hale. Besides Peter Benzanson and George Harvey all of whom resided in the area, George Smith, Martin Sperry, Martin Smith, James Kirker, and John Fleming all received a portion of the Hale grant in 1827.

Thomas Hector emigrated from Edinburgh, Scotland and settled at

Quoddy marrying Catherine Currie. He was involved in shipbuilding and is remembered for building the *Lotus*, the largest brig and second largest vessel to be constructed along the Eastern Shore. Joseph Young was born in the Bras d'Or region of Cape Breton in 1837. As a young man, he joined the Hector Shipyards as a carpenter and married Thomas Hector's daughter, Sarah. They had eleven children. William Isaac Stuart, another resident of Quoddy in 1853, also had eleven children. Mr. Stuart played an important part in the development of the community as a magistrate, farmer, teacher, and shipbuilder.

A scenic view of the small community of West Quoddy. 1999 (AW)

The highway leading into East Quoddy. 1999 (AW)

Harrigan Cove

On the Eastern Shore, approximately thirty-two kilometers north east of Sheet Harbour, lies the community of Harrigan Cove. It is not known whether or not it was named for a settler.

A scenic view of present day Harrigan Cove. 1999 (AW)

By 1801, Charles and Darius Snow of Lawrencetown, Halifax County, were living in Harrigan Cove, the first Snows to settle in the region. They were joined by William Atkins, an Englishman who had originally settled at St. Margaret's Bay in 1819. The Atkins family was involved in the fishing industry and built schooners.

Three members of the Sheir family had arrived by 1838 and their descendants can still be found in the Harrigan area. Joseph Gammon and his wife Susan MacDonald moved their family from Dartmouth to Harrigan Cove in the mid-1850s. He was a blacksmith, deputy sheriff, and gentleman farmer, and many of their descendants still live in the area today.

Gold was discovered in 1868, with gold mining continuing into the beginning of this century. Others who played an important role in the development of the community included Burnham and Morrill of Portland, Maine, who operated a lobster processing factory in 1883, and Archibald and Daniel MacDonald, formerly of Virginia, who by 1893 were building schooners in Harrigan Cove as well as fishing and farming.

MOOSEHEAD

Moosehead, once known as Moose Headland, can be found on the west side of Necum Teuch Harbour. The name originates from the early pioneers who hunted the plentiful animals in the 1790s. Most of those who settled in the community moved from other nearby settlements, usually in search of work. Donald MacDonald was issued a land grant in 1848 and was followed by James Myers in 1880, Neil Moser, Henry Moser, and John MacDonald arriving a few years later.

Off the shore near the community of Moose Head. 1999 (AW)

NECUM TEUCH

Necum Teuch is located about twenty-six kilometers north east of Sheet Harbour. The Mi'kmaq called the area "Noogoomkeak" meaning "soft sand place."

The first family to settle was John U. Smith Sr., the son of George Michael Schmidt who had ventured to Nova Scotia from Palatinate, Germany aboard the ship called the *Gale* in 1752. John Sr. purchased nine hundred acres from George Dunn in 1803 and the settlement, which once included Moser River, was

Replicas of people placed in the front yard of a home in the community of Necum Teuch. 1999 (AW)

originally known as Smith Cove. Mr. Smith soon discovered that the land was not George Dunn's to sell, and so he convinced the government to grant land in 1824 to his three sons, John Jr., George, and Jacob Smith. The family then turned their attention to building schooners in Necum Teuch Bay (Nicumteau Bay).

A scenic view of the Necum Teuch area. 1999 (AW)

By 1827, eight families lived in the community, and as late as 1956 the population had risen to only ninety-eight permanent residents.

Mitchell Bay

On the west side of Ecum Secum Inlet lies the settlement of Mitchell Bay. While it may have been named for an early settler, it was Henry Pye in 1817 who received a two hundred-acre grant in an area the Mi'kmaq called "Ekemsigam." By 1834, it was officially called Mitchell Bay. Other families continued to arrive in the area to settle, including Samuel Bernard and Thomas Worthey.

Mrs. William Jewers, mail carrier and a descendant of one of the Mitchell Bay's founding families. (NSARM)

Ecum Secum

The small community of Ecum Secum lies thirty-two kilometers north east of Sheet Harbour, and is mainly situated in the St. Mary's Municipality of Guysborough County. The name, a variation of the Mi'kmaq "Ekemsigam" was spelled "Ekemsagen" in 1813 and was not spelled as Ecum Secum until 1845.

One of the earliest known settlers was John Jewers (Jure), an

Englishman who had arrived by 1780. Others who came included the sons of Thomas Pye Sr., Thomas Jr. and Henry, who settled in the area around 1817 and raised large families. These families were involved in the fishing industry.

The bridge over the Ecum Secum river leading into the community of the same name. 1999 (AW)

By 1827, those residing in the settlement included the families of Henry Pye, and George, Francis, and Robert Jewers. Descendants still live in Ecum Secum and surrounding communities.

Other settlers included Samuel Barnard, son of Samuel and Mary Barnard of England and Jacob Fleet from Blandford, Lunenburg County. Both families worked in the fishing and farming industry. Many of their descendants still reside in the area today.

Moser River

The Mi'kmaq also called the Moser River area "Noogoomkeak" for "soft sand place." Situated between Necum Teuch on the east and Moosehead on the west, it was once called Necum Teuch River but was changed to Moser River after the Moser family received a land grant.

The road leading into the small community of Moser River. 1999 (AW)

In 1796, Henry and Hannah Moser purchased Foss and Dunn land grants in the Moosehead district which included this area. Henry Moser Sr. was a direct descendant of one of the Foreign Protestants who had settled in Lunenburg County in the mid-1700s. Mr. Moser with his four sons and brother-in-law John Urban Smith settled on the east side of Moser's River. They were soon joined by others from Lunenburg

County, including the Englehutt (Inglehutt), Fraser, Corkum, White, Carr, Oxenham, and Naugler families.

James Croft, who was born in 1859, arrived from LaHave, Lunenberg County in 1880, found work as a lumberman in Moser River and married Fanny Smith of Ecum Secum. Joseph Dimock, son of Alex and Harriett Dimcok of Cornwallis, Kings County, settled in Moser River and in 1871 married Alice E. Moser. He held the mail contract from Moser River to West River Sheet Harbour for nine years, from 1888 to 1897.

It was the lumber industry that attracted many of these settlers to Moser River. Companies such as Brownwell Lumber, McMann Lumber of New Brunswick and Albion Lumber operated in the community and surrounding area for a number of years during the latter part of the 1800s.

Lochaber Mines

Lochaber Mines is located on the Sheet Harbour River, northeast of the village of Sheet Harbour. Named after Lochaber in Scotland, Lochaber Mines was first settled by a Scotsman named Fraser in 1812. Other Scottish families that lived in the vicinity for a number of years included the Lowes and Camerons. A number of families from nearby communities also moved into the settlement, including the Malay, Russell, McCarthy, McDonald, Beeswanger, and Bezanson families.

The river near the rural community of Lochaber Mines prevented from flowing freely due to the dam constructed near Malay Falls. 1999 (AW)

Gold was mined by J.H. Anderson in the latter half of the 1880s, and he built a road to the mine from Sheet Harbour Road. By 1912, the gold was depleted but the road helped to improve lumber operations and soon lumber replaced gold as an important economic resource for the residents.

Malay Falls

North of Sheet Harbour lies the rural community of Malay Falls. Once a part of the Sutherland grant or "Soldier's Grant," the area included a number of neighbouring communities. It was named for the Malay family, one of the first to settle in the region, although it was known as Salmon Falls in 1849 during the time the Cameron family received a 100-acre grant.

A dam was constructed to help in the production of electrical power for the residents of Malay Falls and other communities. A number of local men pitched in to help with construction, including some with the names of Fisher, Coady, Currie, Logan, Lowe, and McCarthy.

The offices of the Nova Scotia power plant established at Malay Falls. 1999 (AW)

In 1923, a power plant was erected to supply power for ground wood pulp mills. There was deep concern about the East River Bridge. The plant contractors were not sure that the bridge could withstand the weight of trucks and materials that needed to be transported across it. From the east end, machinery on a sled was slowly dragged across the bridge by eight double horse teams. Then in 1938, the J. Lewis and Sons Lumber Company transported a nine tonne sawmill boiler across the bridge without any problems.

The building of the power plant must have been quite a sight. Cement was moved on model T Ford trucks that had been purchased without their steel bodies. Instead, wooden boxes were fitted to the trucks and they were driven by Peter Glawson, Earl Behie, Austin Frost, and William Rutledge. These same trucks, once they were no longer needed, were hauled to the Union Dam site where the wheels were removed and replaced by "flanged steel wheels" to run on steel rails.

Operations continued into the summer and winter. Under ice and snow, horses and sleds were used to move cement and other construction materials.

Residents of the community worked at the Malay Falls hydro plant, some as engineers and others as supervisors. They included individuals from the Fultz, Fellows, Anderson, Grant, MacKenzie, Russell, Marshall, and Henley families. Among the men who patrolled the storage dams were Joseph Crowell, Angus MacPherson, and Joseph, Urban and Colin Malay. All of these names are associated with the building of the dam and the power plant as many of these families still reside in the area and nearby communities.

Liscomb Sanctuary

Located at the Eastern edge of Halifax Regional Municipality, Liscomb Sanctuary was established in 1928 under the direction of W. L. Hill, then Minister of Lands and Forests. It lies half in the old Halifax County and half in Guysborough County and can be accessed by route #374. It is the largest wilderness preserve in Nova Scotia.

A sign indicating the entrance to the Liscomb Sanctuary. 1999 (AW)

To help those who might become stranded, warden camps have been established at various points along the route, each stocked with food, firewood and other basic survival supplies. Camps can be found at Fifteen Mile Stream, Sandy Island, Governor Lake, and Long Lake, all within the Sanctuary. There is also a road leading from the settlement of Trafalgar in Guysborough County to the south gate of the sanctuary. The area is a favourite playground to those who enjoy canoeing, hiking, fishing, birdwatching, and snowmobiling.

Chapter Six

Musquodoboit Valley Area

- Pleasant Valley/Sheet Harbour Road
- Chaplin, Dean
- Hutchinson Settlement
- Moose River Gold Mines
- Caribou Gold Mines
- Upper Musquodoboit
- Elmsvale
- Higginsville, Newcomb Corner, Brookvale, Murchyville
- Middle Musquodoboit
- Glenmore
- Chaswood
- Cooks Brook
- Elderbank, Meagher's Grant
- Wyses Corner
- Antrium

The highway leading to Trafalgar, in Guysborough County. 1999 (AW)

Introduction

This chapter explores the Musquodoboit Valley, a fertile farming area of scattered rural communities and farms, some located along dirt roads. The area extends from the rural communities of Chaplin and Dean, not far from Upper Musquodoboit, past the gold mining towns of Moose River and Caribou to the settlement of Antrium, along the Old Guysborough Road from the Halifax International Airport. In the centre of the valley is Middle Musquodoboit, one of the larger areas. The village is home to a community centre and an annual agricultural fair.

Most of the settlers who received grants along the valley were originally from Scotland or Ireland. Some had fought for the British during the American Revolution and arrived as Loyalists. But one influential group was a handful of farmers from the Truro area who discovered the valley while on a hunting trip, and removed their families to farm the fertile soil of the Musquodoboit Valley. Besides lumbering and farming that are still being carried on in the valley, new resources are being discovered. In 1995, Kao Clay Resources Inc. began the process of developing various grades of kaolin, a type of clay, especially those suitable for producing paper, thus increasing the economic future of the valley area.

Pleasant Valley/ Sheet Harbour Road

Overlooking Mill Lake and situated a short distance within the woodlands off of Highway #224 are the communities of Pleasant Valley and Sheet Harbour Road. Pleasant Valley expresses the scenic beauty of the countryside. Early settlers conjured up a less pastoral image, by referring to the area as Pinch Gut.

The story behind that name concerns the Archibald family whose food supplies ran perilously low during one long, cold winter. In order to survive, the family had to conserve food and "pinch their guts."

Highway #224 is also referred to as Sheet Harbour Road as it leads across the municipality to Sheet Harbour. By 1816, two families had settled in the area: John Laidlaw and Mrs. Elizabeth Irvine of Halifax. Moses Redmond and Alexander Murray joined them in 1827, followed by Thomas Richards in 1829.

A scenic view of the Beaver Dam Lake area. 1999 (AW)

Further along the Sheet Harbour Road is a small settlement known as Beaver Dam Lake. The area is one of several Mi'kmaq reserves in Nova Scotia with approximately sixty Mi'kmaqs residing in the area.

Chaplin, Dean

Chaplin is a rural community located in the Musquodoboit Valley along Route #336, close to the Colchester County line. It may have been named for an early settler. The families of Gustavus Stupert and John Chubb were living in the region by 1811. Nearby, another rural community is named for the Dean family who settled here in 1798. Most of the earlier settlers farmed in order to feed their families, although lumbering operations were developed later during the nineteenth century.

Chaplin Pioneer Cemetery where a number of the founding families lie buried. 1999 (AW)

Hutchinson Settlement

Hutchinson Settlement is situated south of the Musquodoboit River, approximately five kilometers east of Mill Lake. Named for an early settler called Hutchinson, the community was once part of the Fisher family's gran, which, in 1780, included the Upper Musquodoboit area.

Moose River Gold Mines

Moose River Gold Mines attracted international attention in April 1936 as the site of the first on-going live radio broadcast of a mine disaster. Dr. David E. Robertson, Herman Russell Magill and Charles Alfred Scadding of Ontario were trapped underground for ten days when an old mine shaft they were investigating collapsed. After six days, rescuers managed to drill a borehole to the men and were able to supply them with food, water, and telephone communications to keep them informed about rescue efforts. It took another four days of digging a tunnel through shattered rock before they could reach the men. Unfortunately, by that time Herman Magill had died, but David Robertson and Charles Scadding survived. A cairn was erected at the site of the first borehole as a memorial to the three men and to commemorate the bravery of the rescue teams.

The stone cairn, erected on the original site where first contact was made to the three men trapped in the Moose River Gold Mine disaster of 1936 with the bore hole still visible at the bottom of the cairn. 1999 (AW)

Moose River Gold Mines is an isolated community, sixty-four kilometers north east of Dartmouth and accessible only by a partially paved road known locally as the Moose River Road. Gold was first discovered here in 1866 by lumbermen working in the area. But it was ten years before the gold was mined. The first gold mining land grants were issued to J.W. Hill in 1874 and 1876.

In 1881, the Moose River Gold Mine Company was established to search for gold. As mining operations got underway, prospectors arrived, among them Dumas Lonquoy who received land grants around Long Lake in

Rescuers communicating with the three men entombed underground during the Moose River Gold Mine disaster in 1936. (NSARM)

1888. By the early 1900s, most of the gold rush was over and Moose River Gold Mines was again an isolated village of only a dozen or so houses. Still the search for gold didn't cease until after the collapse of the mine in 1936.

Today a number of waste banks (holes filled with water) serve as a reminder of the gold mining years. Although hazardous, they are marked by fences. In 1986 the area was made into a Provincial Park with picnic areas and large quartz boulders visible around the site. There is also the Moose River Gold Mine Museum, located in an old schoolhouse on the Moose River Road exhibiting documents about gold mining in the region and the mine disaster.

Caribou Gold Mines

Caribou Gold Mines is a community situated along a dirt road off the Moose River Road. It is named for the caribou that once roamed in the area, as well as for the gold discovered in 1864. The Mi'kmaq called it "Kalebooakade," which means "caribou place."

There were a number of families residing in the area before the discovery of gold, among them the Ryder, Keith, Fairbanks, and Maynard families, as well as Leopold Burkman, Andrew Deckman, and Ebenezer Fulton. But by 1868, just four people lived there: Charles Turple, the postmaster, James White and Robert Wright, both miners, and John Watson, a farmer.

By the 1870s, other families had arrived, many of them employed in the mining industry. They came from all over and included the Jennings, Diller (Irish), Wilson (Scots), Touquoy (French), Dechman, Burris, Turple (German), Miller, Butcher, Kennedy (English), Horne, Brodie, Ryder, Keith, Fairbanks, and Maynard families. Many of the lakes in the surrounding countryside received their names from these families that settled here during the 1800s.

Caribou Gold Mines was a bustling mining village until the gold became depleted and families moved away. From time to time, new mines were developed or old mines reopened, with new settlers arriving. Among them the Logan, Hilchey, Rankin, Brown, Sanford, and White families. The community built a church and a school and for awhile there were a few business enterprises. But as new settlements were established nearby many of the original settlers and their families moved on. Without the gold mines, there was little employment. The rocky soil made farming difficult and although trees abounded, there was no easy means of hauling them out of the forest.

But in the spring of 1874 and the fall of 1875, thirty-eight Icelandic families were brought here to form a new settlement between Mooseland Gold Mines and Caribou Gold Mines, in an area referred to as Markland. They included families by the names of Johnsson, Solvason, Tonison, Hillman, and Brynjolfsson, to mention only a few. They named their farms, according to Icelandic tradition, from the landscape surrounding them. The farm "by the brook" was known as "Arbakki," while the "Lundar" farm "stood near a grove."

The Icelanders were given the necessities for farming, a log cabin and a school for their children. Living in such isolation they had no choice but to try to farm, though a few helped build the Moose River Road. After seven years of struggling with the rocky soil and tree stumps, the families decided to move west to Manitoba and North Dakota. In 1883, the majority of the Icelanders boarded a train in Halifax, with only a small number remaining. Among them, was Sigretha (Sarah) who married Porter Taylor of nearby Chaswood. Their descendants still live in the municipality. A group of residents have formed the Icelandic Memorial Society of Nova Scotia and are in the process of erecting a cairn in honour of the memory of the Icelandic settlement and to encourage the descendants to preserve their heritage.

Today only four families live year round in Caribou Gold Mines—Cody, Garnier (nee Murphy), Watson (nee Logan), and Belmore. Other families own cottages or summer camps, including the Power, Watson, Evan, McKinnon, Logan, Brown, Redden, and Burrow families.

Upper Musquodoboit

The word "Musquodoboit" is the anglicized version of the Mi'kmaq word "Mooskudoboogwek," which means "the road that runs over the hill." Along Route #224, there were once three communities connected with the name of Musquodoboit. Upper Musquodoboit, which stands at

Upper Musquodoboit with the road on the right leading to Sheet Harbour along the Eastern Shore. 1999 (AW)

Musquodoboit Rural High School. 1999 (AW)

The entrance to the MacTara Lumber Company in Upper Musquodoboit. 1999 (AW)

the crossroads of Route #224 and Highway #336, Centre Musquodoboit (now Elmsvale), and Middle Musquodoboit.

For awhile, Upper Musquodoboit was referred to as Fisher's Grant, after one of the first families to receive a land grant in the area. In the spring of 1784, a group of pioneers arrived from the Truro area to take up farming. They included the families of John, James, and Samuel Fisher, Stewtly (Stutley) Horton, who was married to Hannah Fisher, Thomas Reynolds, John Holman, and Robert Geddes. Apparently, some members of this group discovered the fertile farming land while on a hunting expedition and decided to apply for a 5,500-acre grant.

Today, Upper Musquodoboit consists of several small commercial enterprises, a community centre, credit union, fire department, school and grocery story. At the outskirts of the village, in an area formerly referred to as Greenwood Settlement, is the MacTara lumber mill, owned by Hugh Erksine, believed to be the biggest sawmill in Nova Scotia.

Elmsvale

Elmsvale, along Route #224, near the Musquodoboit River, was first known as Centre Musquodoboit; its name change reflects the elm trees that grow in the region. But the earliest settlers called it simply, "The Flat." Among the first settlers were three Archibald brothers who arrived in 1786; they were part of the hunting party from Truro who discovered the fertile Musquodoboit Valley.

Higgins Settlement, Newcomb Corner, Brookvale, Murchyville

Located near Lindsay Lake, not far from Middle Musquodoboit is the small rural community of Higgins Settlement, also known as Higginsville. It was named for the Higgins family, prominent members of the community. John Higgins Sr. fought for the British during the American Revolution, and he and his wife and nine children arrived in Nova Scotia as Loyalists. In 1810, John Higgin's three sons, John Jr., George, and James, also settled in the community and nearby Newcomb Corner, along with the MacLeod and Dykeman families, who arrived in 1812. Twelve more families received grants totalling 3,200 acres in 1814.

Farming still plays a major role in the development of the economy in the Higginsville area. 1999 (AW)

Newcomb Corner, south of the Musquodoboit River, is named for Judson Newcomb, the postmaster for the area in 1868.

Brookvale, about forty kilometers south east of Truro, was known as Mill Village or Reid School Section until 1871. One of the first to arrive in the area was John Lindsay who received three hundred acres in 1812 when the community was part of the Middle Musquodoboit grant.

Murchyville is situated in dense forest close to Higginsville and many of the descendants of John Higgins and John Nelson moved to the area. Along with Brookvale, this small community was first called Mill Village prior to the Scots settling here around 1812, including one family by the name of Merson. It was called Murchyville after the post office was established in 1876. Today this small community is becoming a busy mining area as gypsum is being extracted from the earth bringing greater economic prosperity to many.

This church is situated at the crossroads leading into the quiet rural area of Newcomb's Corner, and has played a major role in the lives of the people of the community. 1999 (AW)

Middle Musquodoboit

The village of Middle Musquodoboit, in the heart of the Musquodoboit Valley, is located near the shores of the Musquodoboit River about thirty-seven kilometers south east of Truro. To the Mi'kmaq it was known as "Natkamkik" meaning "the river extends uphill."

The Scots were among the first to arrive here around 1790. Like many of the other early pioneers along the Musquodoboit River, they were from the Truro area of Colchester County. Finding the land along the river more fertile, they sold their Truro farms and resettled in the valley. Alexander MacNutt Fisher inherited his father's Truro farm, sold it, moved to Middle Musquodoboit and married a local girl, Janet Archibald in 1798. The Archibald family—David, Matthew, and Thomas—were among the first seven families to build homesteads in the area.

A photograph of a long time resident, Sarah Jane Sprott of Middle Musquodoboit. (NSARM)

Many of the descendants of families who moved to the Musquodoboit Valley at the turn of the nineteenth century still reside in the area. Johann Casper Faulkner (Volcher) arrived in Nova Scotia as one of the Foreign Protestants. His son Bernard Faulkner, who married Mary Baker, settled in several different communities prior to coming to the Musquodoboit area. James Dean, who married Margaret Johnson of Truro in 1805, arrived around the same time. William Fisher, son of William and Esther Fisher, settled in the Musquodoboit Valley as a blacksmith and married Kezia Holdman in 1810. Thomas McCollum, son of David and Margaret McCollum of Truro, arrived in the valley, married Janet Logan, and raised seven children. The Anderson family arrived in 1819 with family members working in the lumber industry and becoming active in politics.

Many of the smaller communities that surround Middle Musquodoboit are named for the families who settled there. In some cases, the names of the settlements have been changed but older residents often use the old names. Kent Settlement, located on the Musquodoboit River about thirty-four kilometers from Truro, was named for the Duke of Kent, father of Queen Victoria. It was first settled by the Archibald brothers, John and Matthew, who arrived in 1786 to establish sawmills.

The buildings and exhibit areas of the Halifax County Exhibition. 1999 (AW)

Nearby Reynolds Settlement was part of the original Fisher grant and was named for Thomas Reynolds, one of the original seven grantees. Fraser Settlement, thirty-eight kilometers of east Truro, is believed to have been named for Alexander Fraser, another Scottish settler.

Middle Musquodoboit is a focal point for residents of the largely rural Musquodoboit Valley. In the early 1980s, the old Oddfellow Hall, constructed in 1928, was renovated and re-emerged as the Bicentennial Theatre. Today, the theatre situated in the centre of the community provides a venue for special events, craft fairs, dances, plays, and musical entertainment. The village is also host to the Halifax County Exhibition, held every August. One of the most popular country fairs in the province, the Exhibition provides local farmers an opportunity to show off their livestock and prize-winning vegetables and flowers, and for residents to view each others crafts, baking, and creative handiwork.

The small village of Middle Musquodoboit, with the various businesses situated in the centre of the community. 1999 (AW)

The former Oddfellow's Hall, now the Bicentennial Theatre located in the village of Middle Musquodoboit. 1999 (AW)

Near Middle Musquodoboit is the Musquodoboit Forestry Centre, operated by the Department of Natural Resources on land donated by the McCurdy family. This educational centre provides visitors with an insight into the development of the local forestry industry. Sawmills are still active with the Taylor Lumber Company producing their own electricity to operate the mill by burning bark and sawdust shavings to heat the boiler and run the turbines.

Also nearby is the Musquodoboit Valley Provincial Park, located on Route #224, forty-two kilometers north of Route #7. The park, which stretches through some parts of the Musquodoboit Valley and along the Musquodoboit River, offers a number of hiking trails.

GLENMORE

The rural community of Glenmore is situated near Middle Musquodoboit. It is believed to be named for either a place in Kilkenny, Ireland, or for the village of Glenmore on the Thames River near Windsor, England.

The first land grants went to Samuel Nelson, and James and Jeremiah Murphy in 1814. The McFetridge family from Ireland arrived in 1816 after surviving a shipwreck off the coast of Cape Breton. After five days and nights spent clinging to a rock, James McFetridge decided to tie a rope around himself and swim to shore. He then helped others to safety. Eventually, he moved to the Musquodoboit area, settled on Joseph Lawson's property in Glenmore, and married Mary White of Brookvale. Members of his immediate family moved to nearby communities, but his son, Samuel, stayed on the family homestead. Other survivors from the same shipwreck eventually settled in various communities in the Musquodoboit Valley.

CHASWOOD

The rural community of Chaswood is situated at the crossroads, located north of Middle Musquodoboit on the Colchester County line. Chaswood has had several different names over the years, including Gays Road River, Taylor Settlement, and Taylorville. Taylor refers to Captain

George Taylor of Banffshire, Scotland, who received a land grant in 1814. He married Helen Simpson and they had thirteen children; some of their descendants still live in the area.

Others who received grants included Thomas Duncan, a Halifax surgeon who decided to return to Scotland and turned his land grant over to a relative James Cassidy. Francis Layton, originally from Yorkshire, England, arrived in 1774 and settled near Chaswood. His eldest son John moved to Upper Musquodoboit but his three remaining sons stayed in the area and established a number of commercial enterprises. Others who came over the years included families with the surnames of Corbett, Wilson, Annand, Cassidy, Lawson, Bogg, and McFetridge.

Late in 1899, villagers decided to rename the community Chaswood in honour of Charles C. Wood which was officially changed by an Act of Legislature in 1901. He was the first soldier killed in the South African War (Boer War) on November 10, 1899. Captain Wood's father, Captain J. Taylor Wood, a great-grandson of US President Zachary Taylor, is known for skillfully piloting the American ship the *Tallahassee* through the narrow Eastern Passage in Halifax Harbour to escape being captured by the Confederates. He became a prominent businessman and was buried in Halifax's Camp Hill Cemetery in 1904.

Cooks Brook

The small rural community of Cooks Brook, just over three kilometers north of Middle Musquodoboit, received its name from William Cook, one of five settlers who shared a grant of 1,700 acres issued in 1786. Today it's a quiet farming community.

Elderbank, Meagher's Grant

At one time, Elderbank, Nuttle Hill, and Meagher's Grant were known collectively as Little Musquodoboit.

Elderbank was also called Bruce's Settlement, after the family who settled there in the late eighteenth century. The Bruce family, together with Thomas Noonan who arrived in 1786 and John Storey who came a few years later, were among the first to live in the area. The village was officially renamed Elderbank by an Act of Legislation in 1912. The name is derived from what may be the oldest church in the Musquodoboit Valley, the St. Andrew Church of Elderbank, a Scotch Presbyterian church which was erected at the top of Nuttle Hill in 1886. Today it is called the St. Andrew's United Church.

St. Andrew's Church was constructed in 1886 and is believed to be the oldest church in the area. 1999 (AW)

Nuttle Brook and Nuttle Hill are named for Willoughby Nuttle, who arrived in the area in 1790.

Meagher's Grant, on Route #357 not far from Musquodoboit Harbour, is believed to be named for Martin Meagher, an Irish Loyalist who received a grant of 5,000 acres in 1783. Meagher arrived in Nova Scotia from North Carolina and was among the Loyalists shipwrecked off Cape Breton Island. A number of other families followed, among them the Blue, Ogilvie, McDonald, Crawford, Byer, Schenk, Dillman, Nix, Fraser, and Stangell families. Roland MacDonald a Loyalist and John Dunbrack a Scotsman from Truro, arrived in 1777. John Ogilvie from the State of Georgia

A scenic view of the rural area of Elderbank with cows grazing in the pasture. 1999 (AW)

arrived in 1783 and was followed in 1790 by Miles McInnis of North Carolina.

By 1884, John Henry Meagher, a distant descendant of Martin Meagher, the original settler, was still living in the area with his wife and six children. He was a nephew of John Meagher, the father of two young girls who became lost in the woods. The story is retold in the poem, "Babes in the Woods" and has been the subject of numerous newspaper articles.

The headstones belonging to the Meagher's family of Meagher's Grant, including the two young sisters known as the "Babes in the Woods" who are buried in Woodlawn Cemetery. (1999)(AW)

Tragedy struck on April 11, 1842. John Meagher was in bed with the measles. His wife was tending a newborn baby. The two sisters, Margaret, aged four, and Jane Elizabeth, just six, wandered off into the densely forested woods close to Lake Loon. By late afternoon when the two children had not returned, a hired hand went to look for them. Their father got out of his sick bed and joined neighbours in a frantic search for the little girls. Their bodies were found April 17, just over three kilometers from their home. They had huddled together, trying to protect each other from the elements and wild animals, but they had died of exposure. The hill on which they were found is known as Melancholy Mountain and is situated not far from Lake Major. The two girls are buried side by side in Dartmouth's Woodlawn Cemetery.

John Henry Meagher's land was sold to Charles Preeper in 1925 and he resided on the farm until the mid-1950s.

WYSE CORNER

Wyse Corner, nearly forty-two kilometers north east of Dartmouth on the Old Guysborough Road (Highway #212) leading past the Halifax International Airport, was first settled by William Wyse who was issued land in the Dollar Lake area. Most of the settlers in the region were involved in lumbering and farming, though some manufactured the hoops coopers needed to finish barrels. At the crossroads, between the Old Guysborough Road and Lake Egmont Road, land was granted to Samuel Bevie in 1814.

The sign indicating the entrance to Dollar Lake Provincial Park, near Wyses's Corner. 1999 (AW)

Among the first settlers were Christopher Dillman and his sons Alexander, John, and Thomas. In 1790 they received land that is now a part of Dollar Lake Provincial Park. The park, which takes in 2,400 acres of crown land, was established in 1981. The park consists of two hundred campsites and visitors can rent canoes and paddle around the lake enjoying the pleasant serenity of the area.

ANTRIUM

The small community of Antrium can be reached by travelling along a dirt road off route #357, near Meagher's Grant. Some of the earliest land grants in this area were issued in 1816 to John McMichael and John Kerr from Antrium in Northern Ireland—hence the area's name. Later, John and James Ogilvie, James Edward, and Robert Sutherland built homes in the community that they previously called New Antrium.

John Kerr and his wife Ann were among the first families to settle here. An enterprising man, Kerr built a sawmill, blacksmith shop, and schoolhouse. His grant was located on the Old Guysborough Road, which was constructed as a route to the Guysborough settlement near Canso.

John's son James married Jane Mullin and built the Kerr Inn near Antrium Crossroads. A number of local teachers boarded at the inn and travellers used it as a stopover on route to the Musquodoboit Valley. The Kerrs also ran a grocery store, post office, and farm.

By 1830, there were twenty-five families living in the community. Nearby were a lumber and shingle mill owned by Nelson Blois. He and his wife, a MacMullan, had a large family and many of their descendants can still be found in the Antrium area. Nelson's father Daniel Blois, was a poet as well as a blacksmith. It was he who penned the poem, "Babes in the Woods," which told the story in verse of the two little Meagher girls lost on Melancholy Mountain in 1842.

Chapter Seven

Waverley to Hants County Border

- Wellington/ Fletcher's Lake
- Fall River
- Windsor Junction
- Waverley
- Goffs
- Grand Lake
- Oakfield
- Enfield
- Oldham
- Devon
- Dutch Settlement

ɪeautiful homes now surɔund the shores of Lake ʼhomas located in Fall River. ʼ999 (AW)

Introduction

This part of the Halifax Municipality stretches from the picturesque suburban villages of Fall River, Wellington, and Waverley, past the Halifax International Airport to the rural farmlands that abut the Hants County line.

Those who settled closer to Halifax and Dartmouth tended to be large landowners, such as Colonel John W. Laurie who brought farmers from Devonshire, England to turn his estate at Oakfield into a major agricultural centre. Those who lived in more remote rural areas tended to work family farms or turned to other trades.

Wellington/Fletcher's Lake

The community of Wellington on beautiful Fletcher's Lake is located north of Halifax on Route #2. Landowner, Colonel John W. Laurie of nearby Oakfield, suggested the name in honour of the Duke of Wellington. A land grant was given to William Shaw in 1784 with John Lees, John Gay, and James Oram following shortly after.

The district was first known as Fletcher's Bridge, after William Fletcher Sr. who purchased land around the lake that bears his name. His son Robert, who also lived at Fletcher's Bridge around 1795, tried to claim his father's property but had some difficulties obtaining title to the land. He did, however, receive a grant in 1812 for land that bordered the road from Halifax to Truro. That same year, two Halifax merchants by the name of Cochran each received five hundred acres in the same general area.

A scenic view of Fletcher's Lake, named for the Fletcher family who first settled its shores. 1999 (AW)

Over the years, Wellington developed into cottage country. Original summer cottages and cabins were later winterized as residents began to live in the district year round and commute to jobs in Sackville, Bedford, Halifax, or Dartmouth.

FALL RIVER

The picturesque village of Fall River, located about twenty kilometers north of Halifax, takes its name from the falls that once flowed from nearby Miller Lake to Lake Thomas. Construction of the Bicentennial Highway in the late 1960s altered the flow of the water and today there is just a trickle of water that flows through a culvert under the highway, near Miller Lake.

Some of the earliest settlers in the region arrived as Loyalists after the American Revolution. They took up land grants near Shubenacadie Grand Lake (now known simply as Grand Lake), one of the largest lakes in the municipality. The lake forms part of a chain of lakes, rivers, and streams that were used by the Mi'kmaq as an overland waterway from Halifax Harbour to the Minas Basin.

During the early 1800s, the Fall River district was referred to as Fletcher's Station or Fletcher Bridge since the community then included what is now Wellington and the Lake Thomas area. The lake received its name from Lieutenant Charles Thomas, cousin of Governor John Wentworth and a friend of Prince Edward, Duke of Kent.

Among the first pioneers to receive land in the community was Daniel Miller in 1785. It was the Millers who not only named Fall River, but gave their own name to Miller Lake at the top of the original falls.

Two Miller brothers, Philip and John, built a dam across the falls in 1828 to power the community's first sawmill. The Miller Lake Dam was later used to power machinery for the Waverley Gold Mines and to operate a lumber mill and the Charles P. Allen chair factory. Other businesses and families moved into the area and soon the mills were producing hand racks and pails for settlers.

Emily Miller, sister to the Miller brothers, married a Suel Brittan who came north from the United States in 1840. It was he who was responsible for introducing many of the various types of fruit trees still growing in the area today.

Henry Forester arrived on the Miller's doorstep in 1840, desperately looking for work. The brothers took pity on him and hired him on at the mill, but soon discovered he was quite an educated gentleman. Henry

Forester married one of John Miller's daughters and went on to become a respected teacher.

By the mid-1800s, five or six mills were working at full capacity to produce wood products that were shipped to the United States. But a trade dispute between Canada and the U.S. around 1878 cooled relations between the two countries and the trade relationships soon declined.

Today the community is a mixture of residential and vacation homes as the modern highway system makes it possible for homeowners to commute to work.

Windsor Junction

North of the Bedford Basin and situated between Second and Third Lake is the small community of Windsor Junction. One of the first families to settle in the area in 1765 was Joseph Scott. It was at this junction in 1867 that the main railway line from Truro to Dartmouth crossed a branch line to Wind-sor. Built by Irish and German settlers, the station and the railway have played an important part in the lives of residents.

The small rural community of Windsor Junction with the railway tracks still visible leading across the centre of Nova Scotia on its way to Truro and beyond. 1999 (AW)

In 1938, the railway transported an Anglican Church from Pictou to the village of Windsor Junction. It must have been quite a sight. Even the church bell was originally once part of a locomotive engine.

Although many of the passenger lines have closed in recent years, the Windsor Junction line is still working, bringing people through the community to the town of Truro, just as it did in 1867.

WAVERLEY

The village of Waverley (formerly known as Germantown) is located approximately eleven kilometers north east of Bedford. The community of Waverley owes its name to Charles P. Allen's love of the literary prose of Sir Walter Scott. One of the earliest residents in the area, Allen named his cottage "Waverley" after the title of one of Scott's novels.

The Waverley Museum, a former church located near School Street in the center of the village. 1999 (AW)

In 1776, about 1,700 acres of land were granted to non-commissioned officers and sailors, including the Corbett, Hilliard, Allen, Bigby, Gray, Greece, and Taylor families. John Allen, who had been living in Halifax by 1812, moved to Waverley to establish a chair factory that would eventually be owned by his relative, Charles Allen.

Waverley's gold rush began in 1861. Cornelius Blois and Alexander Taylor, while scouting around the eastern edge of a pond near the Allen property, discovered gold deposits. Shortly after James Skerry discovered more gold in the eastern half of the village. Within four years, the Waverley Gold Mining Company was in operation, with miners brought from Germany and Cornwall in southwest England. Mining went on for nearly 40 years, but by 1903 the gold was nearly gone and the mine was shut down. There was a slight reprieve in the early 1930s and for a short period gold was mined once again. Other industries took its place. A number of mills and factories were established, including the Acadia Powder Company, which manufactured dynamite for mining operations and the Tudor Mining Company. In 1926, the Waverley Game Sanctuary was established on the south side of Miller Lake.

The history of the area is being preserved by the Waverley Heritage Society, which operates the Waverley Heritage Museum in a former church on Rocky Lake Drive. Inside, visitors will find gold mining artifacts, pictures of school children, archival and sports records, a stamp-mill model, and blacksmith tools, to chronicle the history of the village of Waverley.

Waverley Road, prior to being paved, winds its way through the rural communities. (NSARM)

Goffs

Goffs, about twenty-eight kilometers north east of Halifax, is situated at the beginning of the Old Guysborough Road, which connects a number of small communities to the county of Guysborough.

The first land grants in the Goffs region were issued in 1784, mainly five to seven hundred acre lots destined for military officers in the British army and government dignitaries and their families. Most recipients looked on their grants as investments and never bothered to settle on them.

In 1812, three Goff brothers received land grants. One brother, Thomas, was issued one hundred acres on the Guysborough Road and was the only brother to remain in Goffs. He built a farmhouse, married Eleanor Holland, daughter of Anthony Holland the founder of the *Acadian Recorder*, settled down to raise ten children and bestowed his name on the area. The former farm is now a nine hole golf course called "Airlane's Golf Course."

Land was also granted to the Polluck family who built the Polluck

Inn (former Thirteen Mile House) in the early 1800s. Many a famous person spent a night or two at the inn, including, in 1861, Edward, Prince of Wales, who went hunting in the area. Arthur and Sarah (MacDonald) Wilson bought the inn from her father William MacDonald around 1900. The Wilson's demolished it and erected a family home in its place. The property stayed in the Wilson family for several generations.

The runways of the Halifax International Airport, which now covers the former lands of the first Goff settlers. 1999 (AW)

Other families arrived over the years. Michael and Catherine Smith came from Ireland in 1812 with their two children. Their daughter Catherine married Henry MacDonald who had purchased land from Theophiles Chamberlain in 1830. For the next one hundred years, three generations of MacDonalds stayed on the farm.

Golfers enjoying a round of golf at the Airlane Golf Course situated on the former farmlands of the Goff family. 1999 (AW)

In 1846, Thomas Goff's son William received land and built Goff's Inn, a popular coach stop for travellers on their way to or from Guysborough. William Goff is also remembered for the beautiful handcrafted furniture he made, some of which may be found in homes today.

Others who came included Captain John William Coote, an Irishman and a widower who arrived in Halifax in 1849 with two young sons and his other twelve remained in Ireland. He built a home on a 500-acre grant near Miller Lake, remarried and had a daughter who married a MacDonald. Many of her descendants remain in the community. Michael Bone of England, a former sergeant in the British army, arrived in 1847.

William and James Topp of Scotland arrived in the 1850s to set up a blacksmith shop. Sometime later, Irishman James Mulligan built a home considered to be unusual for the times. He attached outbuildings to the main house in the European style. Not long after, came Michael Riley, another Irishman who specialized in successfully planting orchards in rocky soil.

Much of the original settlement of Goff now lies under the paved runways of the Halifax International Airport constructed in 1960 and the nearby 2000-acre AeroTech Industrial Park, which opened in 1985 and is one of the fastest growing business parks in the province. The Old Guysborough Road now passes by woods and scrub, dotted with a few old farmhouses, although some of those old buildings are now slowly being replaced by modern bungalows.

Grand Lake

Grand Lake (formerly Shubenacadie Grand Lake) is part of that same chain of lakes that the Mi'kmaq used as an overland waterway. They called it "Tulugadik," meaning "camping ground." The community of Grand Lake borders the lake of the same name on Route #2.

In the early 1800s, the Kenty family of Truro received a land grant and moved to Grand Lake area to set up a sawmill. They were followed by the Kirk family in 1813 and then by John Bazalgette and a number of others who shared a land grant of 2,265 acres.

Matthew Adam's camp was once situated on the shores of Grand Lake. (NSARM)

Close to the community is Laurie Provincial Park, a 60-acre park located on land donated by K.C. Laurie. He was the son of Colonel John Winburn Laurie who owned the estate situated nearby in Oakfield. The park was opened in September 1961 with picnic areas, camping sites, walking trails, and a swimming area to be enjoyed by tourists and residents alike.

The entrance to Grand Lake's Laurie Provincial Park showing a cairn erected as a memorial to the Laurie family. 1999 (AW)

OAKFIELD

Oakfield, on the east side of Grand Lake and about thirty-two kilometers from Halifax, was the name of the estate once owned by Colonel John Winburn Laurie. He named it for the numerous oak trees found on his property.

The Laurie family had been living on Morris Street in the south end of Halifax when Colonel Laurie decided to buy about 800 acres on Grand Lake. On a visit to Devonshire, England to see his eldest son, a Member of Parliament for Barnstaple, he decided to bring Devonshire farmers back to Nova Scotia to work his estate. He offered each family a house and a barn and had hopes of setting up a thriving agricultural farm.

A sign indicating the entrance to the Oakfield Provincial Park, situated on the lands donated by the Laurie family for the establishment of a recreational area. 1999 (AW)

Soon the small community was a self-sufficient village with a tannery and a lumber mill. Colonel Laurie built a schoolhouse in 1875 to educate the farmers' children. He also provided his workers with a small wooden chapel, which has been enlarged over the years.

The Colonel returned to England in 1889 and leased his farm to James Chipman, a horse breeder. Over time, others leased the land and continued to provide employment for the villagers until the death of Colonel Laurie in 1912. The home remained in the family until Laurie's son died in 1962 at the age of eighty-six. A year later the church that Colonel Laurie had built was given to the Anglican Diocese of Nova Scotia. Several members of the family are interred in the cemetery located beside the church.

A Notman portrait of Lieut. Colonel L. Winburn Laurie (1835-1912) in full military dress, taken ca. 1902. (NSARM)

Today the Oakfield Provincial Park is situated on Grand Lake where Colonel Laurie established his agricultural farm. It was officially opened in 1961, and a plaque stands as a memorial to the Laurie family. Designated picnic areas are situated along the open fields and a large grassy area is available for group events. A small beach and walking trail are accessible as well as a place to launch boats.

ENFIELD

The village of Enfield is situated mainly in Hants County with a small portion in Halifax Regional Municipality.

It was first settled by disbanded British soldiers, but soon Irish, German, and Highland Scots were building homes in the village. Legend has it that one Englishman, outraged by the number of foreigners in the area, harnessed a horse to ride to Halifax to see the King's official. Once there he supposedly banged his fist on a table and demanded the village be named Enfield, a name that reminded him of England.

Jacob Horne of Quebec was a Prussian soldier who had distinguished himself on the battlefields of the Plains of Abraham in 1759. In recognition of his efforts on behalf of the British, he was given his choice of lands in Nova Scotia. He chose Eastern Passage. However, his son Andrew settled down with his wife Barbara Gephard, a German from Dutch Town near Halifax, and raised fourteen children in the Enfield area.

Andrew's children established farms in a number of surrounding communities. Philip became a blacksmith in Elmsdale. Thomas settled in Oldham while Andrew moved near Enfield and established Horn Settlement. He divided his property among his children who eventually dropped the 'e' from Horne. The cemetery at Enfield lists the deaths of a number of Horn family descendants.

The annual Jack Jones Memorial Race being held on the Nine Mile River near Enfield. 1999 (AW)

OLDHAM

On the rural road between Enfield and Goffs lies the village of Oldham, named by Joseph Howe for the birthplace in England of his ancestors.

Gold was found here in 1861 and Edward Horne, together with Samuel Isnor soon established mining operations, along with eight crushing mills erected by 1863. Prospectors and their families arrived, followed by mining officials and tradesmen. Soon the roads were improved and houses, saloons, general stores, churches and schools were built. For a number of years it was quite a prosperous little town.

As with so many places in Nova Scotia, the gold petered out, the prospectors left and the town's residents had to find other means of employment or move on themselves. Many left, of course, such as some of the early settlers, the Greenough and Vandergraft families, while others moved to nearby communities to settle including the Davis, Fraser, Wright, Ferguson, and O'Shaughnessy families. You will still find the descendants of the Cole, Graham, Horne and Whidden families living in the region.

The highway leading through the small rural community of Oldham. 1999 (AW)

DEVON

Devon is a small rural community about thirty-two kilometers north of Dartmouth and not far from Goffs. It is believed that Devon was named for Devonshire, England, possibly by some of those Devonshire farmers who worked on the Oakfield estate.

Two of the earliest settlers who arrived in 1810 were the Thompson and Heffernen families. Not long after Thomas Cox, an Irishman who had served with the British Army, arrived to operate a farm along the newly constructed Guysborough Road. He was also employed by the Royal Mail to deliver the post.

In 1850, Edward Robertson Poole from Ireland and his wife Myra (Hogan) and their five children settled on the road behind the schoolhouse. Edward Poole, an engineer, was hired to help with construction of the railway lines between Halifax, Windsor, and Truro.

A paved highway winds its way through the woodlands surrounding the small rural community of Devon. 1999 (AW)

William Preeper, arrived in 1860 and established one of the most prosperous farms in the community. He and his wife Mary Ellen had twelve children. William Preeper also delivered mail and took in school teachers as boarders. A small lake in the vicinity bears the Preeper name.

Dutch Settlement

Dutch Settlement is located north east of Halifax on the Shubenacadie River, off of Route #277. The present name of the community originated from the fact that a number of Germans moved to the area and once again the word "Deutche" was anglicized to "Dutch."

Among the first to arrive was William Keys (Keyes) in 1786, and the area was called Keyes for a short time. Soon the population grew as German families from the Lunenburg area continued to arrive. They had first moved to St. Margaret's Bay before moving on to an area better suited to farming. They were joined by a number of Irish families.

By the 1800s, George Brown had settled in the area. He was followed by George Eisenhauer (Isnor), Charles Hines, and George Grosrenaud (Grono) in 1817 from St. Margaret's Bay. They were the first families to purchase land that had been part of the original Keys land grant. Around 1838, Thomas Logan from Ireland arrived with his family.

Logan had fought for the Americans in the War of 1812 and had been captured and imprisoned in Halifax. After the war he returned to Ireland, then came back to Nova Scotia bringing several members of his family with him in 1838.

By 1839 a number of new families had arrived in the community, with such names as Curry, Parker, Philip, Wordrope, and Wilson as well as the Corbett, Logan, and Ashley families. Oliver Simpson, an Irishman, arrived later than the others in 1875.

Not far from Dutch Settlement is Carrolls Corner, named for Louis Carroll who settled on one hundred acres in 1792. In the early 1800s, other families arrived including those with the surnames of Bowlby, Logan, Lord, and Bell.

The dirt road leads to a small community named for the Carroll family called Carroll's Corner. 1999 (AW)

Chapter Eight

St. Margaret's Bay Area

- Hubbards
- Queensland
- Black Point
- Ingramport
- Boutilier's Point
- Head of St. Margaret's Bay
- Lower and Upper Tantallon
- Hammonds Plains, Upper Hammonds Plains, Pockwock, Lucasville
- Lewis Lake
- Hubley
- Glen Haven
- French Village
- Seabright
- Glen Margaret
- Hackett's Cove
- Indian Harbour
- Peggy's Cove

On the Hammonds Plains Road, near the former site of English Corner, where the road to the right leads to the small rural communities of Upper Hammonds Plains and Pockwock. 1999 (AW)

Introduction

Much of this area covers a stretch of land from the village of Hubbards on the Lunenburg County line, along the head of St. Margaret's Bay and down the scenic route #333 to the famous lighthouse at Peggy's Cove. It also includes part of the Hammonds Plains Road, which joins Bedford Basin with St. Margaret's Bay.

The early settlers who lived on the bay turned to fishing as a way of life. These early settlers were predominently descendants of Foreign Protestants who had settled in Lunenburg County around

1753, and Loyalists who arrived around 1785. Farther along Hammonds Plains, at Lucasville and Pockwock, are a number of Black communities whose residents are descendants of the freed Chesapeake Blacks who came to Canada after the War of 1812.

HUBBARDS

The village of Hubbards, formerly Hubbards Cove, was most likely named for an early settler though no proof of this has been found.

During the 1790s, Gottlieb Harnish of Lunenburg purchased 650 acres of land from the Arenburg family who held it as a land grant but had never settled in the region. Later, in 1820, Captain John Dauphinee, who had been residing across the bay at French Village, purchased some

Members of the Hubbard's Tuna hockey team ca. 1930. L to R: Charles and Jack MacLean, Rev. George Ernest, Harry Harnish, Albert Dorey, Margerson Jollimore, Fred MacLean, and Guy Harnish. (NSARM)

of the Harnish land that became known as Dauphinee's Point. At one time, Hubbards boasted a number of hotels and inns. Now all are gone, except for the Dauphinee Inn, which is owned by descendants of Gottlieb Harnish.

A portrait photograph of Amelia (Boutilier) Dorey, Rebecca (Boutilier) Nauss, and Margaret (Boutilier) Applin, taken ca. 1898. (NSARM)

Other families settled in the area, among them were the MacLean, Shankel, Shatford, Slaunwhite, Dorey, and Kean families. Some of their descendants still live in the area.

Most communities have their storytellers who pass down local legends and folklore through the generations. Some of these stories are true while others may be pure fiction. The story of a family legacy bestowed on this community by one of its former residents is decidedly true. At the turn of the century or earlier, J.D. Shatford, one of the Shatford boys, decided to try his luck in the United States. His father gave him a cheque to help him on his way and apparently J.D. decided to add a few extra zeros to the cheque. Over the years, J.D. acquired a fortune as an industrialist in the corporate world. He never returned to Hubbards until after his parents had died. When he died he left the town a large legacy on the understanding that the money would be used for educational, religious, and recreational purposes only. Part of his bequest has helped two important local institutions named in his honour: the J.D. Shatford Memorial Public Library and the Shatford Memorial Elementary School.

The Hubbards Heritage Society is very active in preserving the history of the community and nearby areas. It organizes various events to help families learn about the community and the pioneers who first came here through storytelling weekends, walking tours, and other activities. They also collect old memorabilia, pictures, and artifacts.

QUEENSLAND

East of Hubbards village is the small community of Queensland, first known simply as North Shore. But in 1901, in honour of Queen Victoria's Jubilee, the community officially changed its name to Queensland.

John F. Slaunwhite (Slawenwright or Schlagentweit) was one of the first settlers who arrived in 1814, along with Jacob Harnish, John Dorey, and John Brigley. The Slaunwhite, Harnish, and Dorey families are descendants of Foreign Protestants who settled in this community but many of their children moved to other parts of the bay, as well as to the city of Halifax.

Within the community is Queensland Beach Provincial Park, a popular swimming area during summer months.

A scenic view of the popular Queensland Beach ca. 1927. (NSARM)

Black Point

Over two hundred years ago, if you had approached Black Point from the bay you would have noticed that the dense trees along the shoreline shrouded the land, giving it the appearance of being black. From this, the Point got its name. The name became established in 1867 when the first post office was established at the home of Ephraim Hubley. Many of the families who settled in the community were descendants of the Foreign Protestants of Lunenburg County.

Members of the James Slaunwhite family, ca. 1905 of Black Point. (NSARM)

Alexander Hubley was one of the first to arrive. He built a home in the early 1800s that is still standing today. It is constructed of trees that stood on his land and is held together with wooden pegs. Inside are hand-hewn beams and in one room there is a hole in the ceiling where the spindle of the spinning wheel was placed. When the roof was renovated it was found that Mr. Hubley had used birchbark beneath the shingles to keep it watertight. Birchbark has also been used inside the walls as insulation. The house was once a way station for travellers breaking their journeys between Chester and Halifax.

Snair's Bakery was first established during the early 1940s by Roy Snair who offered meals with homemade rolls and bread. 1995 (AW)

Black Point is largely residential today, with a few commercial enterprises and a fire station. There is a stone cairn at Black Point Beach, placed there in 1985 by the Bicentennial Committee, to commemorate the arrival of the early settlers. Among those families whose descendants still live in the community are the Hubleys, Snairs, Slaunwhites, Langilles, Jollimores, and Culps.

INGRAMPORT

The rural community of Ingramport on the northwest side of the bay received its name from Charles Ingram, one of the first settlers who lived near Ingram River that now also bears his name. He had been a sergeant with the Warburton Regiment and was stationed in Halifax in 1749. Others who arrived included the Crawford and Brown families in 1763, followed by the Westhavers in 1834.

Lumber stacked on the Lewis Miller Company's wharf in Ingramport ready to be shipped to far away places ca. 1900. (NSARM)

A fire engine, off the railway tracks, was brought to Ingramport from Halifax to help fight the fire that destroyed the Lewis Miller Lumbering Company in 1928. (NSARM)

In 1905, the name of the community officially became Ingramport. One of the more prosperous industries to flourish at Ingramport was lumbering. In the early 1900s, the Lewis Miller Lumbering Company was established. Ships arrived from around the world and the company provided work and affluence to many residents, including the Swedish settlers brought to Ingramport by the company. But as the forests were stripped, the lumbering operations came to an end. Many workers moved elsewhere and today Ingramport is largely a rural residential community with a few homes and some summer cottages.

Boutilier's Point

Boutilier's Point, twenty-eight kilometers from Halifax, was first settled by the family of James Boutilier prior to 1815. He was a descendant of the Foreign Protestant Boutiliers and was considered the patriarch of the community. Due to the numerous "Boutilier" families in the area, it became common practice for a person to be known by his given name plus that of his father. For example, John the son of Jack Boutilier became known as John Jack.

Three members of the Boutilier family shearing sheep ca. 1930. L to R: Sandy Boutilier, Douglas Boutilier and Nellie (Boutilier) Christie. (NSARM)

The Boutiliers were not the only settlers. Others who arrived included the Dauphinee, Munroe, Croucher, Garrison, and Slaunwhite families. The Garrisons were Loyalists who immigrated around 1785. The Crouchers, of Irish ancestry, had first settled in Newfoundland. Samuel and James Croucher lived with their families on Croucher's Island, just off Boutilier's Point.

The early settlers had to clear land that seemed to be mostly granite rock so that they could plant a vegetable garden for their families. While a few residents farmed, others were employed at the Lewis Miller Lumbering Company in Ingramport or were involved in the fishing industry. Most communities have their share of folklore and ghost stories Boutilier Point is no exception.

A young couple, Ellen Garrison and Donny Troop, were married in the local Anglican Church according to her faith, even though the groom was a Methodist. Not long after their marriage Ellen died, and Donny arranged for her to be buried in the Methodist graveyard near his home so that he would always have her nearby. The evening of her burial, eerie sounds could be heard throughout the community. They seemed to be emanating from the Troop farm but whenever anyone approached, the noises mysteriously stopped. Then a green glow was seen encircling the farm. On the third night, as residents stood watch, the earth trembled and the house shook.

By then, Donny had decided that Ellen might be behind these occurrences. He felt that with her strong religious views she was probably unhappy being buried in his churchyard. He had her coffin moved to the Anglican cemetery and Ellen was never heard from again.

Head of St. Margaret's Bay

Samuel de Champlain, the renowned cartographer and explorer, charted the waters around St. Margaret's Bay in the early 1600s. The bay was named for his mother Marguerite, as it appears as "St. Marguerite Baie" on his map of 1612. At the head of the bay lies the small community appropriately named, Head of St. Margaret's Bay.

In the 1750s, a number of land grants were issued to prominent Halifax families who never settled on their properties. So the land was escheated and granted in 1785 to second generation families of the Foreign Protestants, including those with the family names of Dauphinee, Mason, and Fader. There was also a Mi'kmaq family by the name of Bernard who received a 500-acre grant, but they too did not settle on their land.

Logging operations being conducted in the Head of St. Margaret's Bay area during the early 1900s. (NSARM))

Todd's Island formerly known as Sheep's Island was a prosperous lumbering place. (NSARM)

Most of the people who lived here were involved in the fishing industry. Others began lumbering operations establishing several sawmills during the years that the lumber business flourished.

In the latter half of the 1800s, the community became a popular tourist area. The Mason family built the Prince of Wales Hotel which provided a stopping place for passing mail coaches, offering many prominent gentlemen from Halifax a place for sport and relaxation.

Lower and Upper Tantallon

Upper and Lower Tantallon extends from the Hammonds Plains Road near Hubley Mill Lake, down to the crossroads of Route #3 and Route #333. The area was once a part of French Village, which explains why the area's former train station, now a gift shop, retains that name. The community became Tantallon sometime in the early 1900s, most likely named for the Scottish stronghold of the Douglas family called Tantallon.

Dauphinee family of Upper Tantallon ca. 1927 sitting in their Model-T Ford. (NSARM)

One of the first settlers was John Dofiney (Dauphinee) who received a grant of 260 acres. George Whynaught (Whynot) was issued 500 acres in 1818, while the Harshman (Hurshman) brothers (James and William) each received 250 acres in 1828. The Whynaught family settled on a piece of land that juts out into Whynacht's Cove and is known as Whynacht's Point.

Nehemiah Dorey owned a blacksmith shop and the Slaunwhites established a number of sawmills. The Longard family helped to build the first Seventh Day Adventist Church, just off the Peggy's Cove Road. The old church has since been replaced by a building that is now used for storage.

Nehemiah Dorey's family in front of their home in Tantallon ca. 1915. (NSARM)

Lewis Boutilier of Tantallon singing and being recorded by folklorist Helen Creighton ca. 1950.

Four farmers of Tantallon planting potatoes ca. 1910. (NSARM)

Today the area is largely residential, with a shopping mall and recreational facilities on land previously owned by Lester Hubley.

Hammonds Plains, Upper Hammonds Plains, Lucasville, Pockwock

The Hammonds Plains Road known as Route #216 travels through four communities, from Millview Cove on the Bedford Basin to Upper Tantallon in St. Margaret's Bay. It was named for Sir Andrew Snape Hamonds (Hammond), Lieutenant Governor from 1781 to 1782. It was one of the first roads built by the municipality as part of the route that was to link Halifax with the Annapolis Valley.

Close to Upper Tantallon along the Hammonds Plains Road is Stillwater Lake, a popular area with cottages and a few residential homes.

The Haverstock family home situated on the Hammond's Plains Road was built in 1915. 1999 (AW)

Farther along Hammonds Plains Road to the right is Yankeetown Road. A few more miles the road forks, turning left leading to Upper Hammonds Plains and Pockwock Lake, at an area known as English Corner during the early 1800s. Pockwock is a Mi'kmaq word that means "the place you can go no farther," and was aptly used here as Pockwock's road ends at the lake. Some old documents refer to it as The Great Pock-Quack while others named it Moose Town.

Further along to the left, is Lucasville Road leading to the Sackville community. A number of prominent Halifax merchants were granted land in this area which they did not develop. The lands were then re-offered in 1785 to Loyalist families who settled in an area they called Yankeetown. Among them were the Smith and Hinty families who arrived in 1792, and the Hays, Wallis', and Fizzells who came a few years later. Shortly after, they were joined by a group of settlers known as the Chester Group, second generation Foreign Protestants with surnames such as Boutilier, Besancon, Wambolt, along with the Thomson, Webber, Melvin, and Ellis families.

St. Nicholas Anglican Church on the Hammonds Plains Road with the road to the right leading to the small community of Lucasville and Atlantic Playland. 1999 (AW)

Jean George Besancon (Bezanson), descended from the Foreign Protestants of Lunenburg County, came as one of the Chester Group, and a number of his descendants still live in the region. Bensancon is remembered for having built a ship, named *The Curlew*, several kilometers from water. To set sail, he hitched sixteen yoked oxen to a cradle on runners and one winter hauled his boat over frozen roads to the Bedford Basin.

Another early arrival was the Loyalist, Ebenezer Smith. He arrived from Maryland with his two sons, Ebenezer Jr. and Nathaniel. Ebenezer

Jr. married a local girl and many of his descendants still live in Hammonds Plains. Another family headed by Margaret Worral of Boston, widow of Thomas Worral, petitioned for land for herself and her seven children. The family was active in the affairs of the community and had a prosperous lumbering business at one time. Jacob Haverstock moved to the area and married Nancy Anderson but after her death he remarried her sister Ellen. Altogether, he had sixteen children and his descendants still reside in Hammonds Plains.

The Haverstock, Moren, Hayes, and Smith families operated lumber mills near Pockwock Lake until the lake became a water supply for the city of Halifax. Another of the early residents, the Johnson family, are descendants of Thomas Johnson, a soldier in the Royal Artillery who arrived in the community around 1811. He operated both an inn and a gristmill near the Lucasville crossroad. In 1816, he was appointed victualer for the Black settlers who arrived in Canada following the War of 1812.

These new arrivals were freed Chesapeake Blacks who were granted land along Upper Hammonds Plains towards Pockwock Lake. They included families with the names of Johnson, Wilson, Hamilton, Symonds, Anderson, Mantley, Brown, David, Whylie, Marsman, Jackson, and Ellison (Allison). Many tried to farm but found the soil too rocky and turned to lumbering instead.

Dean Wiley, the grandson of one of the freed Black families, built a mill in 1888 and then purchased barrel making machinery. For many years he and his descendants made the wooden barrels used by many Halifax merchants.

Lucasville covers the small community along the Lucasville Road between Hammonds Plains and Sackville. It was named for James Lucas (Locas), an early pioneer. Other grants during the 1760s went to Richard Wenman and John Georg Pyke. In the early 1800s, a few of the Chesapeake Black families settled along the road. They included those with the surnames William, Parsons, Kelsie, Oliver, and Dishna. There is also a trailer park and a lumber mill, owned by the Heffler family who have operated the mill for generations. Also situated on this road is "Atlantic Playland" where children and adults can enjoy a day of fun with go-carts, water slides, miniature golf, and the arcade.

Lewis Lake

Lewis Lake, just nineteen kilometers west of Halifax on Route #3, was probably named for an early settler. There are still several families living here whose ancestors were among the early pioneers, including the Doreys, Smiths, and Dauphinees.

This is largely a rural area though a new subdivision is being developed. Not far away is Lewis Lake Provincial Park, which offers recreational facilities in an outdoor setting for those who are physically disabled, including a wheelchair look-off, walk-ways, picnic sites, and nature trails.

The entrance to the Lewis Lake Provincial Park on the boundary of the Upper Tantallon and Lewis Lake communities. 1999 (AW)

Hubley

The small community of Hubley was once known as Fourteen Mile House because of its distance from Halifax. It was named for Alexander Hubley, a descendant of Johann Ulrich Hubli. The elder Hubli was one of the Foreign Protestants who settled in Lunenburg County in 1753. Alexander settled in what today is Seabright and often travelled from the Bay to Halifax. He soon recognized the need for a way station between the two communities. Popular mythology has it that one day, as Alexander Hubley was making his way to Halifax to sell produce after a snowstorm, he came across a peddler's pack and footprints leading into the forest. He followed the tracks and soon found the body of the peddler who had frozen to death. Struck by the tragedy of this event, Hubley petitioned for a land grant of one hundred acres to build the

Fourteen Mile House which became a popular stopping place right up until the mid-1900s. Full of entrepreneurial spirit, the Hubley family also organized hunting and fishing expeditions and acted as wilderness guides.

When a train station was constructed in the community at the start of the twentieth century, the area became known as Hubley Station. An Act of Legislation in 1901 had the name changed to Hubley. But in the early 1960s, people began referring to the area as Five Island Lake after a local lake and the Five Island Lake Elementary School. Descendants of Alexander Hubley petitioned to have the name Hubley restored, which has been done on road signs along Highway #103. Today a number of subdivisions have been developed on either side of the highway that cuts through the community.

A stone cairn erected in memory of Rebecca Hubley who donated land for the former Five Island Lake Elementary School to be constructed in 1953 in Hubley now the industrial annex to the Sir John A. Macdonald High School. 1999 (AW)

GLEN HAVEN

Glen Haven is immediately adjacent to Lower Tantallon along Route #333, also known as the Peggy's Cove Road. It was once a part of French Village and was settled by a number of Foreign Protestants from Lunenburg County around 1785. Names such as Boutilier, Hubley, and Dauphinee can still be found in the bay area.

Around 1900, Gordon Hubley organized a petition to create a separate community with a new name—and its own post office. Glen Haven was chosen to reflect the natural beauty of the area.

Within the community is a peninsula that stretches into the bay called Indian Point. At the tip are two small islands: Big Indian Island

and Little Indian Island. All three are so named because of arrowheads and other Indian artifacts that have been found there in the past, suggesting that this was once a Mi'kmaq summer camping ground.

A Notman portrait photograph of Isabella and Henry Garrison of Glen Haven, ca. 1890. (NSARM)

The Eisenhauer (Isnor) family sailing near Glen Haven in 1939, with the Grono family's home in the background. (NSARM)

French Village

At one time, French Village included Upper and Lower Tantallon, Glen Haven, and Seabright, and covered much of the land along Route #333. No doubt this area served as a summer camp for the Mi'kmaq and a story passed down through many generations that the first European settlers to arrive in the region saw several wigwams around the bay. The vil-

Calvin Burchell's fishing wharf in French Village ca. 1950. (NSARM)

lage probably gets its name from the earliest settlers, many of whom were descendants of Foreign Protestants. These names are now familiar: Boutilier, Dauphinee, Dorey, Brine, Langille, Hubley, and Mason. However, there were also several families who were descended from Loyalist settlers. John Burchell of Ireland arrived in the bay around 1850 and married a local girl. His descendants still reside in French Village, some on the old homestead.

The oldest graveyard along the bay, Pioneer Cemetery, is located in French Village. In 1794, James and Susanne Boutilier were paid six pounds for an acre of land to establish the cemetery. In 1974 a list was compiled of the names on the headstones still standing (and legible). Today it is difficult to find the graveyard, which is overgrown with brush, many of its headstones broken and lying in ruins.

SEABRIGHT

At first Seabright was part of French Village. When the Village was subdivided, this land became known as Hubley after one of the first settlers of 1785. But as there was already another Hubley in the same postal area, it was changed in 1902 to Seabright after the local Seabright Hotel. Now vacant, the hotel was once host to a number of celebrities, such as

A scenic view of Wooden's River in Seabright ca. 1910, with the Saddler homestead situated in the center of the photograph. (NSARM)

The Dauphinee family haying on Collishaw's Point, in Seabright ca. 1900. (NSARM)

the American author Zane Grey, Franklin Roosevelt Jr., the Canadian professor and politician Sidney Smith, and King George VI's physician, Dr. Creighton.

Other Loyalists and Foreign Protestants settled in and around Seabright. Such names as MacDonald, Umlah (Hemlock), Wooden, Collishaw, Redmond, Johnson, and Hubley can still be found in the area. The MacDonalds, Redmonds, and Woodens were Scottish families who arrived as Loyalists. The Umlahs, also Scottish, originally came from Philadelphia in 1762. William Umlah and his wife, a MacDonald, had ten children and many of the descendants of these children live in surrounding communities, including Goodwood, in the Prospect area.

Glen Margaret

As the name suggests, the community of Glen Margaret was first settled by Scottish Loyalists, among them John Creighton, Alexander and Hugh MacDonald, and Donald Patterson. Other Loyalists with such names as Renfrew, Moore, Marven, Redmond, and Munroe also settled here.

Fred Fraser's home built ca. 1842 in Glen Margaret. Fraser was a descendant of the first Fraser settler who arrived as a Loyalist, ca. 1925. (NSARM)

This district was first known as Lower Ward. It was later changed to Glen Margaret in honour of the wife of John Fraser, one of the early Scottish Loyalist settlers. In 1801, Fraser purchased much of the land that had been originally granted to John Creighton. He had come from Virginia and had settled in Shelburne with his father and brothers following the American Revolution. After his father died John, who was still a young lad, stowed away on one of the vessels belonging to the Boutilier family that was bringing supplies to St. Margaret's Bay. He was taken in by the Boutiliers and set up in the family's fishing business. He fell in love and married Suzanne, one of Captain Boutilier's daughters. One of the Fraser houses he built still stands in the community. On the chimney is painted a wide black band to signify that the family who lived there were Loyalists.

William Black Memorial Church, Nova Scotia's oldest Methodist Church is located in Glen Margaret. It was erected by the community in 1821 and is now a registered heritage property.

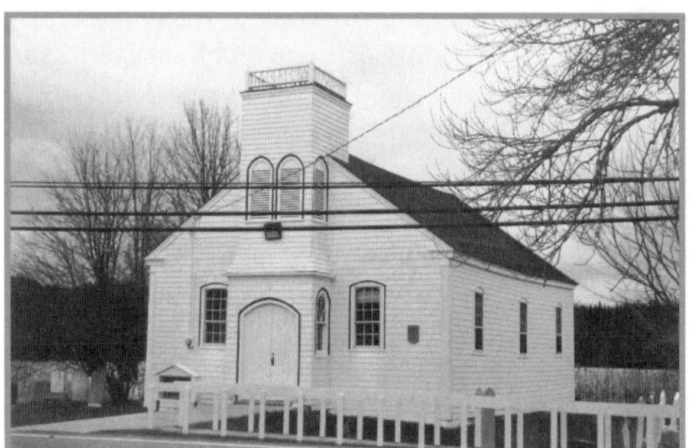

The William Black Memorial Church is believed to be the oldest Methodist Church in Nova Scotia, erected in 1821. 1995 (AW)

Hackett's Cove

Nestled between Indian Harbour and Seabright, along the old Peggy's Cove Road, is the community of Hackett's Cove. It might have been named after a settler called Haggett, but there is no evidence that any such family ever lived there. The name Haggett is found in reference to a school district that existed during the early 1800s. Again, this was an area settled by former Foreign Protestants and some of the names of the families are familiar: Croucher, Adams, Dofiney (Dauphinee), Fralick, Moser (Mosher), Gates (Gatez), and Wambolt (Wamboldt).

Among the Loyalist pioneers was the MacDonald family, originally from Scotland. Hugh MacDonald had fought for the British during the American Revolution and was granted land along St. Margaret's Bay. There is a headstone in the graveyard attached to St. Peter's Anglican Church that states it was erected by Hugh when his mother, Jeannette

A photograph of William and Harriet Covey ca. 1910, descendants of the first Covey settler to arrive in the Hackett's Cove community. (NSARM)

died. It may well be the oldest headstone in the St. Margaret's Bay area.

There is a family story, never confirmed, that these MacDonalds were related to Flora MacDonald, the spirited Highland lass who hid Bonnie Prince Charlie from the English after the Battle of Culloden. The sheets that Jeannette is buried in are said to be the same ones that Prince Charles slept in while in hiding with the MacDonald family on the Isle of Skye.

A scenic view of Boutilier's Cove located in Hackett's Cove ca. 1960. (NSARM)

Today's residents of Hackett's Cove are fishers or are involved in the tourist industry. Others work for NAUTEL Limited, a manufacturer of high power radio frequency products, which was established over thirty years ago.

Indian Harbour

Less than two kilometers from Peggy's Cove, Indian Harbour was once a popular fishing and hunting grounds for the Mi'kmaq.

The community was first settled by the Covey, Allen, and Richardson families. Christopher Allen was a sailor who jumped ship in Halifax Harbour and found his way to St. Margaret's Bay. By 1866, other families were residing in the area, namely the Boutiliers, Manuels, Johnsons, Shatfords, and Corkums. The community is in close proximity to Peggy's Cove so some of the residents realized the benefits of establishing motels and bed and breakfasts to cater to the tourist industry.

A scenic photograph of sail boats anchored in Indian Harbour ca. 1900. (NSARM)

A road leading through the small rural community of Hackett's Cove prior to being paved ca. 1925. (NSARM)

Peggy's Cove

The fishing village of Peggy's Cove at the entrance to St. Margaret's Bay was originally known simply as Eastern Point Harbour because it is situated at the eastern side of the bay. Eventually it was changed to Peggy's Cove, perhaps in honour of the wife of one of the first settlers, an Irishman by the name of William Rogers. Apparently, he did not stay long but moved on to a land grant on Caribou Island in Pictou County.

There is a romantic folk tale that offers another explanation concerning how the cove got its name. Young Peggy was travelling by ship to Halifax to meet her fiancé when her ship floundered on the rocks. She was rescued by local folk who took care of her. When one would go visit her, they would say they were going to see "Peggy of the Cove." Though a nice story, there is no evidence to substantiate either this or the tale of William Rogers' wife. What's more, a deed issued to six families in

James Manuel, a fisherman mending his fishing nets on his wharf in Peggy's Cove ca. 1925. (NSARM)

1809 names the area as Peggy's Cove but records that no one was living there at the time.

Six families—two Troop (Troup) brothers, three Isenhauer (Isnor) brothers, and a man by the name of Kayzer—divided the land around the cove into six lots, which were further divided and now twenty-five families live in the village. Many are related to families in Indian Harbour or Hacketts Cove, with such names as Manuel, Crooks, Croucher, Daubin, and Garrison.

The lighthouse at Peggy's Cove is probably the most photographed in the world. It was built in 1914 and today serves as a post office for tourists during the summer months. The lighthouse is unmanned but the light still burns to warn sailors of the rocky coastline. Peggy's Cove was only kilometers from the site of a tragic plane crash in 1998 in which all 229 passengers of Swissair Flight 111 were killed.

One of Peggy's Cove most famous residents was William deGarthe, an artist and sculptor who had emigrated from Finland. He often came to the cove to paint marine life, the residents of the cove and their way of life. In 1954, he bought a home at the head of the Cove, which today serves as an art gallery displaying his work. He also carved a memorial to the courage of the fishermen living in the cove. The sculpture, which took him ten years to complete, covers a 30-meter granite outcrop of rock in his backyard. Depicted are St. Michael, guardian angel of fishermen, several fishermen, their wives and children, Peggy of the Cove, and deGarthe's pet seagull Joe. The Provincial Government now maintains the upkeep of the William E. deGarthe Memorial Provincial Park.

Fisherman's Monument carved by William deGarthe (1977-1983) near his home in Peggy's Cove is a popular tourist attraction. 1995 (AW)

Chapter Nine

PROSPECT/ TERENCE BAY AREA

- West and East Dover
- Blind Bay, Bayside
- Shad Bay
- Lower Prospect, and Upper Prospect
- White's Lake
- Terence Bay
- Brookside, Hatchet Lake
- Goodwood
- Beechville
- Lakeside
- Timberlea

scenic view of McGrath's ake in Brookside where omes have been constructed the surrounding area over he years, forming a small ommunity of its own. 1999 AW)

This area extends up the coast from Peggy's Cove through a number of small fishing villages along the Prospect Road to the residential communities of Beechville, Lakeside, and Timberlea.

Despite being in close proximity to Halifax, the area didn't develop until the mid-twentieth century and even then many of the early settlers were those who had received land grants elsewhere around St. Margaret's Bay and had chosen to move on. There is an exception at Beechville where a number of Black refugees from the War of 1812 received land grants.

West and East Dover

In 1893 these two communities, roughly twenty-four kilometers from Halifax, were known as Ocean Glen and also included what today are West Dover, McCrath's Cove, and Scott's Point. It took an Act of Legislation to divide the area into East and West Dover. The name Dover was chosen to serve as a reminder to the settlers of the seaport on the south coast of England by the same name. West Dover is situated on the Peggy's Cove Road at the entrance to Blind Bay while East Dover leads from the Peggy's Cove Road down the East Dover Road to McGrath's Cove.

Arthur Isnor of West Dover, proudly displaying a huge lobster found in his lobster traps. (NSARM)

Seven fishermen in front of the lighthouse situated on Betty's Island near the shoreline of East Dover, with Peter Christian and his son, Herbert, standing near the centre. (courtesy of Eva Coolen)

There are a couple of other smaller communities within the general area. At the end of the East Dover Road lies Scott's Point, a tiny fishing village of about thirty homes. And not far from West Dover, just five miles east of Peggy's Cove Road is Middle Village, a rural community of summer homes that have been winterized. It's a photographer's paradise.

Several Scottish families along with a few Irishmen moved to the area. James Carrie received 124 acres in 1855 while the three Fader brothers—Henry, James, and Noah—were issued their grants in 1865, 1866, and 1877 respectively. In 1875, William Burns joined them with a grant of one hundred acres. Other families arrived: the Duggans, Coolens, Tanners, Scotts, Forens, Connors, and Murphys. The Scott family settled at Scott's Point on McGrath Cove along with the Foren and Connor families.

Members of the Coolen family get together for a family outing in East Dover. L to R: Larry and Carrie Coolen, Rich and Mabel Coolen, Alphonse and Charity (Coolen) Petrie, Leo and Mary (Coolen) Lashkow, Annie (Coolen) Guilcher, Bernard and Sarah (Coolen) Murphy, Luke Coolen; the lady in front is unkown. (courtesy of Eva Coolen of East Dover)

In the late 1800s, the communities were prosperous fishing villages with a post office, hotel, schools, and several businesses. The pride of the East Dover village is the magnificent St. Thomas Catholic Church, which was built in 1888. It stands atop solid rock, which had to be blasted by dynamite to ensure the building would not topple over.

Fish houses and sheds located in the East Dover community. (courtesy of Eva Coolen)

A scenic view of Leary's Cove in East Dover taken from the front yard of the Coolen family home. 1999 (AW)

The small picturesque fishing village of McGrath's Cove is just off the road leading to East Dover. 1999 (AW)

Blind Bay, Bayside

The highway winding its way through the small rural community of Bayside. 1999 (AW)

The small community of Blind Bay on a cloudy day. 1999 (AW)

Bayside, on the shores of Blind Bay at the head of Shag Harbour, is just nineteen kilometers from Halifax along Route #333. There is a story that Blind Bay got its name because, at times, the fog rolling up Shag Harbour is so thick it blinds the fishermen in the bay. And Bayside, of course, is so named because it is on a bay.

The Mi'kmaq used to camp nearby in an area called Barkhouse Hill. The hill probably got its name from the Barkhouse family, one of the earlier settlers. But just the same, here the Mi'kmaq used a process involving the bark of trees to prevent their fishing nets from rotting in salt water. They boiled together bark and fish guts until the bark drew the fish oil out of the guts. Then the nets were soaked in the oily solution that acted as a barrier against the seawater.

The first settlers received their grant on February 4, 1764. Daniel George and Peter Marlow were the first to arrive. They were followed by families named Barkhouse, Ernst, Zinck, Fader, Whiston, Longard, Courtney, Balcolm, and McGrath.

A descendant of the Fader family, Fendly Fader, is credited as the inventor of bleach. Despite an absence of electricity he used a water wheel to power the machinery he used to make his product. Sometime in 1939, a Halifax newspaper ran an advertisement offering $5 to anyone who could come up with a name for the product. The winning entry was "Sunny Monday." Monday was the traditional laundry day for most housewives who would hope for sun to dry their washing.

By the 1930s, there were a number of successful enterprises established in the area. Captain Noah Zink (Zinck) owned a shipyard near the bay. One of his ships, a schooner named *Oakleaf*, was constructed entirely of oak trees growing in the region.

The local three-storey hotel, the Bayview, and a lumber mill caught fire in 1935. Wind swept the flames through the village and wiped it out. Some residents, surrounded by flames, had to be evacuated by boat to Shoal Bay on the opposite shore.

Today in Bayside an eighteen-hole golf course, Granite Springs, overlooks the waters of Shad Bay. The sport is popular for both residents and visiting tourists.

Shad Bay

The rural community of Shad Bay, located at the head of the bay was named in 1764 for the abundance of shad fish in the area's waters. However, prior to when the first settlers arrived the area was called Shag Bay.

The first family to receive a land grant was the Marlows. In 1810, William Fawson and John Carter were issued grants that included Shad Harbour River and Middle Island, located near Middle Village. Thirty-three years later the Marlow grant was divided and the Red-

The newly renovated Government Wharf in Shad Bay with Cochran Island (formerly Weeping Widows Island) seen in the distance. 1999 (AW)

mond and Collier families moved into the community. In 1872 Thomas Coolen arrived, followed by William Davies of Halifax in 1892.

Near Shad Bay is Cochran Island. It was once known more poignantly as Weeping Widows Island. As legend has it, the pirate Captain Kidd buried his ill-gotten treasure on the island. He ordered forty-three men to dig two pits. Once the treasure was buried he slaughtered his workers and sailed off with the forty-three weeping widows. Today at low tide this is a favourite spot for picking mussels.

During the 1930s and 1940s, it was popular for Halifax firms to hold company picnics on nearby Coolen's Beach. For many years the beach was surrounded by summer cottages, many of which, over the years, have been winterized.

Shad Bay was once an active fishing village; today it is better known for its recreational boating and swimming.

Lower Prospect and Upper Prospect

Upper Prospect is located at the end of a twelve-kilometer road that leads off of Route #333, Lower Prospect is on the opposite side of Prospect Bay, a little closer to Terence Bay. The Mi'kmaq knew the area

A scenic view of the small fishing community of Prospect Village ca. 1920. (NSARM)

as "Nospadakun," meaning "a herb mixed with tobacco." Nearby Coolen's Hill was once their summer camp.

As early as 1672, the Acadians were calling the area Passepec. By 1693 it was referred to as Paspek or Paspec, then in 1744 it became Prospec. It didn't become Prospect until the British settled here in 1754.

Mr. Saul, a fisherman from the Prospect area. (NSARM)

From the top of Coolen's Hill, you can see a number of beautiful islands known as the "Barra Soie." Between them and the mainland is a narrow passage known to sailors and yachtmen as "The Roost."

A few of the families to arrive in the Prospect area were descended from the Foreign Protestants of Lunenburg. But most were of Irish origins: the Brophy, Christian, Connor, Coolen, Duggan, Kiley, Mullins, O'Brien, Powers, Redmond, Shea, and Purcell families.

Mr. Power, the postmaster and a descendant of the first settler of the Power family to arrive in Prospect Village. (NSARM)

In Prospect Harbour is Calatian Island, which was granted to the Connor family in 1787. Timothy Mullins had been living in Nova Scotia for over thirty years before he received a land grant in 1788 that included Mullins Island. William Coolen had been in Newfoundland, then at the Halifax garrison before he moved his family to a land grant in Prospect around 1808. The Powers family arrived in 1811. Roger Power was a fisherman and his home still stands close to the old post road that leads down to the Government Wharf.

At one time, it may have been used to house the militia during the Fenian Raids during the mid-1800s. The Fenians who were an Irish nationalist secret society dedicated to achieving independence from Britain, were involved in the so-called Fenian Raids, cross-border skirmishes by American-Irish Fenians into British Canada between 1866 and 1871.

Two Irish families—headed by Patrick Purcell and James Shea—arrived in 1816 at Upper Prospect, known also as Prospect Village. Patrick Purcell was a merchant who had been living on a nearby island for over twenty-five years before he finally received title to his grant. James Shea had been living in the area for thirteen years. Others who arrived included Dennis Brophy, a sergeant in the Nova Scotia Regiment who was granted a fishing lot in 1819, and James O'Brien who arrived with his wife and nine children in 1831. By 1851, John Brophy and family were living in what is today Lower Prospect. In the mid-1870s, William and Nicholas Christian and James Coolen all received grants and settled in the community.

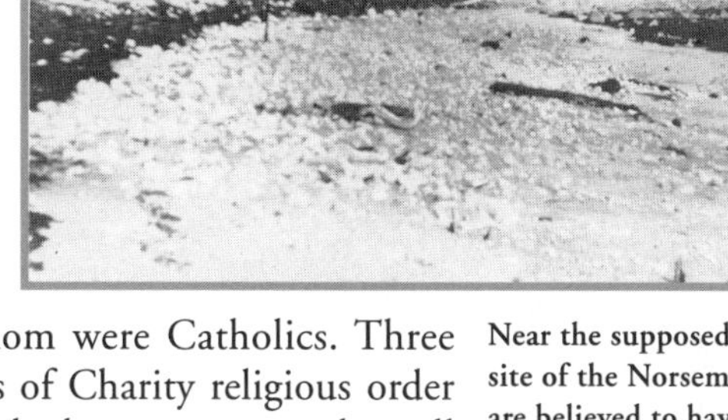

Near the supposed landing site of the Norsemen who are believed to have arrived long ago upon the shores of Prospect Bay. (NSARM)

At one time, Prospect had a population consisting of three thousand fishermen and their families, most of whom were Catholics. Three nuns from the Sisters of Charity religious order arrived in 1876 and had a nunnery and small chapel erected that doubled as a schoolhouse. The nunnery was restored as a hotel by the Young family, and today is a bed and breakfast establishment.

According to popular legend, a conch shell was sounded each day at twelve noon and the people would stop whatever they were doing to say their "angelus"—five minutes of silent prayer.

By the early 1900s, Prospect was quite a prosperous fishing village, with a number of recreational facilities, including a bowling alley, tavern, and bowery for holding social functions, church suppers, and dances.

Today some fishing remains while visitors enjoy a nearby sandy beach, sea canoeing, or walks along designated trails. Off the coast of Prospect is Betty's Island. The small island is surrounded by granite boulders and was named for the daughter of Samuel and Joanne White, one of the island's first families to settle here. Originally, the lighthouse was located on top of the lighthouse keeper's home. The structure has been protecting fishermen from crashing upon the rocks for over one hundred years. Many residents of Prospect Village, as well as other nearby communities, have played a role as the island's lightkeeper.

White's Lake

White's Lake is a small community on Prospect Road approximately nineteen kilometers southwest of Halifax. White's Lake was most likely named for the White family who settled in the area sometime in the

The highway leading through the small community of White's Lake with the road on the left leading to the Terence Bay area. 1999 (AW)

early 1800s. Others soon arrived. with John Christian settled on his 97 acres around 1835, joined in 1847 by William H. Rudolph who had received a grant of 120 acres. Michael Hogan was there by 1850, and a year later James Duggan moved to the community. Others who arrived over the last one hundred years include the Beazley, Church, and Power families.

Some of the families established mills at the point where the waters of White's Lake River flow into Prospect Bay, among them Josh Church. Jeff Christian operated a slaughterhouse at the corner of Terence Bay and Prospect Roads. In about 1930, Roy Christian opened the first Texaco gas station in the region, ran the post office, and acted as a Justice of the Peace.

There are still a few commercial enterprises and subdivisions being developed in the community today as many of its residents commute to work.

TERENCE BAY

The village of Terence Bay is thirteen kilometers off of the Prospect Road and will be forever remembered for the fateful night of April 1st, 1873. On that day the SS *Atlantic*, en route to New York with a number

A scenic view of the fishing village of Terence Bay. (NSARM)

A scenic view of the road prior to being paved leading from White's Lake to the village of Terence Bay. (NSARM)

The cairn erected in memory of the 562 victims who died when the S. S. *Atlantic* sunk on April 1, 1873, near the Terence Bay/ Prospect Bay coastline. (NSARM)

John H. Hindley, the only child survivor from the tragic sinking of the S.S. Atlantic in 1873 near the Terence Bay/Prospect Bay shores. (NSARM)

of immigrants, turned back towards Halifax to replenish its coal supply. The ship struck the Marr's Rock formation off Terence Bay and floundered. Some passengers were able to climb on to nearby rocks while others were swept back out to sea by the rolling waves. No women and only one child survived the disaster. When news of the tragedy broke, volunteers came from as far away as Halifax to offer assistance to the survivors. There is a cairn there now as a memorial to those who lost their lives, and efforts are underway to protect the graveyard where many victims are buried, from being exposed to the elements or washed into the sea.

It is difficult to determine how the village got its name. Over the centuries it has been called Terrants Bay, Tern Bay, Turner Bay, and Turner Bay Rock. Much of the land was granted in 1852 to John Brophy, James A. Moren, Patrick McGloan, and the families of Drysdale, Slaunwhite, and Jollimore. Some were Irishmen, others Foreign Protestants. The Slaunwhites (Sch-lagentweit) originated from Wurttemburg, Germany while the Jollimores (Jolimois) came from Montbeliard, France.

A photograph of the sinking of the S. S. *Atlantic* on the rocks near Terence Bay/Prospect Bay in 1873. (NSARM)

Some of the Slaunwhite family took their fathers' Christian names to serve as their surnames because of the confusion resulting from so many Slaunwhites living in the area. John Slaunwhite, son of Harry Slaunwhite, became John Harrie, with the descendants continuing to use the surname "Harrie" today.

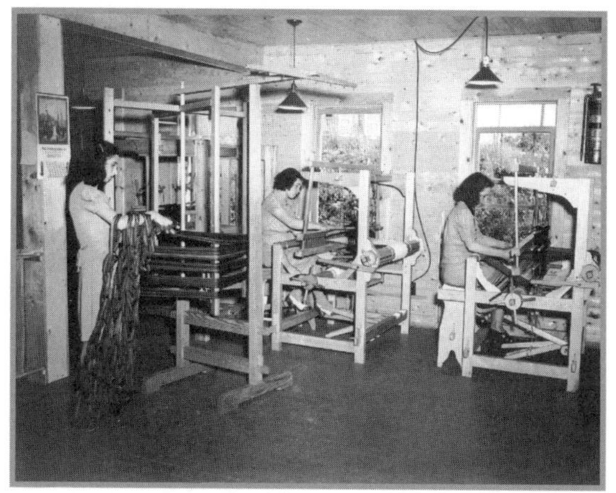

Inside the Terence Bay Community Centre with three young women weaving handcrafts to raise money for the village in 1941. (NSARM)

In 1938, the Roman Catholic Sisters of Charity arrived in the village and built a convent the next year. Within a few years they had a flourishing handicraft and woodworking business generating employment for many of the residents. Today Terence Bay is a quiet rural village.

Brookside, Hatchet Lake

Located near McGrath Lake, just fourteen kilometers from Halifax, Brookside is a quiet residential neighbourhood. In 1787, John Drysdale and the Parker, Nicols, and Drysdale families received a 1550-acre grant among them. Later in 1817, William Drysdale arrived, after being discharged from the army, to live on his grant of two hundred acres. Other families moved into the area, including W.D. Yeadon who arrived in the late 1880s. Today the community is blended in with Hatchet Lake and is made visible only by the Brookside Road that leads to the original settlement.

The Prospect Road winds its way through the small community of Hatchet Lake. 1999 (AW)

Hatchet Lake, a small rural community that now includes Brookside, is located on Prospect Road. The area may have been named for a pioneer who lost his hatchet or it may be because the lake is said to somewhat resemble the shape of a hatchet. This community was also part of the 1550 acres issued to several families in 1787, in connection with Brookside.

Goodwood

South of Ragged Lake on the Prospect Road, less than seven kilometers from Halifax, is the community of Goodwood. This descriptive name had been used prior to the first land grants being issued in 1775 to John Gosbee, Thomas Wagner, John Bower, and Phillip Tollmer.

The Drysdale and Umlah families arrived some time during the 1860s. The Drysdales consisted of several brothers and their sons, including Charles, James Sr., James Jr., William, and John. There are descendants of some of the first settlers still living in the area.

Goodwood is largely a rural residential area surrounded by dense woodland. It is also home to the Atlantic Exhibition Park where a number of trade shows and the annual Atlantic Winter Fair are held each year.

Descendants of John Umlah who received land in the Goodwood area ca. 1860, now part of the Long Lake Provincial Park. (MSHS) (courtesy of the late Ruth Miller.)

The buildings which form a part of the Atlantic Exhibition Park situated in the small rural community of Goodwood. 1999 (AW)

BEECHVILLE

Near the beginning of the St. Margaret's Bay Road is the village of Beechville, once situated among beech trees, was first known as Beech Hill. After the War of 1812, several land grants were issued to Black families, including those with the surnames of Allen, Hamilton, Lovett, Cooper, and Roberts, each of whom received ten acres.

Many of the earliest arrivals were refugees who had escaped from slavery from the southern American colonies. They played their part in the War of 1812 and were given a grant of five thousand acres near the North West Arm in a section that came to be known as Refugee Hill. The area, which was comprised of the Chain Lakes to the Nine Mile River and Beech Hill, became known as Beechville.

By 1851, families named Davis, Roberts, Maxwell, Ryan, James, Allan, and Creaser had settled in the area. The Baptist Church played an important role in the development of the community and in 1868, a baptism was recorded in local newspapers in which forty-seven people were baptized in Lovett Lake while over one thousand stood in attendance. The event became known as "The Great Baptism," which was later commemorated in a poem and painting. Lumbering operations were carried out in the vicinity of Nine Mile River and the various lakes found within the community. Today Beechville has blended in with the other communities along the St. Margaret's Bay Road. However, this small community is now in the process of expanding as a new subdivision, along with a new state-of-the-art school under construction.

A photograph of one of the newly developed subdivisions within the Beechville community with the Ridgecliff Middle School in the process of being constructed. 1999 (AW)

LAKESIDE

Lakeside is a small community situated between Beechville and Timberlea along the St. Margaret's Bay Road. The name of the area is derived from its location, near Governor Lake. Land grants were issued to Theodosius Morris in 1846, to William Donovon in 1896, and to J.S. Hubley in 1905. The community borders the Lakeside Industrial Park and is not far from the Bayers Lake Industrial Park.

TIMBERLEA

Timberlea was first known as Nine Mile River after the river that flows through the village. For a short period of time the community was named Bowser Station around 1905 after Angus Bowser, a postmaster and hotelkeeper. The community was renamed Timberlea in 1922 by which time it was a busy lumbering and sawmill centre.

In Timberlea, a former site of the Fraser family's sawmill, once situated near Fraser's Lake with St. Andrew's Anglican Church now situated near the site. 1999 (AW)

The Boutilier family, descendants of Foreign Protestants who had previously settled in the St. Margaret's Bay region during the late 1700s, moved to the area and received a 650-acre grant. The family had already begun cutting a road through the wilderness when George Boutilier settled here in 1821, soon to be followed by John, Peter and Jacob Boutilier in 1822.

John Fraser of Glen Margaret arrived in 1830 to build a sawmill near what today is Fraser Lake. He operated a cordwood business during the winter and returned to Glen Margaret for the summer. Then, Cyrus

Boutilier was given fifty acres in 1841 and erected a second sawmill in the community. Others who moved into the area included the Umlah, Moore, Martin, Lambert, Rhuda, Johnson, Pace, Troop, Potts, and Isenor families.

Logging operations and sawmills continued to fuel the economy for a number of years. George Fraser bought the Boutilier lands and manufactured wooden boxes along with his sons Aubrey, Robert, and Charles. The business flourished until the 1950s. The Poirier family moved to the area to construct homes that they sold to new residents. They formed one of the first contract business enterprises in the community.

Today Timberlea is largely residential, offering affordable housing within easy commuting distance of Halifax. In 1958, the Poiriers started the Parkdale Heights Subdivision while the Isnor family organized the Greenwood Heights Subdivision. Timberlea Hills, now known as Glengarry Gardens, and Timberlea Village have been developed over recent years.

Chapter 10

Sambro/ Purcell's Cove

- Harrietsfield, Williamswood
- Pennant
- Sambro, Sambro Creek, Sambro Head
- Bald Rock
- Ketch Harbour
- Duncan's Cove
- Portuguese Cove
- Herring Cove
- Ferguson's Cove
- Purcell's Cove
- Jollimore
- Spryfield

A scenic view of Herring Cove Village around the early 1900s. (NSARM)

This part of the municipality begins in Harrietsfield, travels along the old Sambro Road, to the coast at Pennant, then along the coastal entrance of the Halifax Harbour, past Ketch Harbour, Portuguese Cove, and Herring Cove, before swinging inland again to Spryfield. The communities along the Old Sambro Road are largely rural, though today they are within easy commuting distance of Halifax. Those who lived in the villages along the coast made their living from fishing or by acting as pilots for ships entering the treacherous Halifax Harbour. This stretch of coast was also part of Halifax's nineteenth century defense systems from the first signal station at Duncan's Cove to the fort at York Redoubt.

Harrietsfield, Williamswood

Harrietsfield, about ten kilometers south of Halifax along the Old Sambro Road (Route #306), was probably named for the wife of Colonel William Thompson, who was living in the area by the 1780s. In 1790, Casper Gruber arrived, and by 1827 there were at least nine other families in the community.

Today this is a largely rural residential area, with access to Halifax along the Old Sambro Road. There are a few commercial enterprises, schools, several churches, and a fire hall, as well as a trailer park which was developed about thirty years ago. The population of the community has been increasing slowly over the years, thanks, in part, to the expansion of the Williamswood area, located near Harrietsfield.

Students of Harrietsfield School trying to remove a rock from the school yard ca. 1939. Clockwise from the top: Bob Whitehead, Robie Vatcher, Mildred and Stan Nickerson, Veda Vatcher, Eric, Marie, and Ruth Salmonson. (MSHS) (Courtesy of Veda Smith)

Pennant

At the head of Pennant Harbour and near Sambro Village, lies the small community of Pennant, named by the early settlers after a village in Wales. The Mi'kmaq called the area "Skabank," meaning "where they eat raw food."

Pennant Point beyond Pennant Harbour was first settled by an Irishman by the name of William MacCarthy. He had bought the land from James Fawson. The Embley and Keating families were the first pioneers to reside near Pennant Harbour. By 1829, they had been joined by Andrew Henneberry and William Osbourne, who were harbour pilots. Ships' captains needing assistance in navigating the rocky entrance to Halifax Harbour would put out a request for a pilot. Both Henneberry and Osbourne would rush to their boats and row over. The first to reach the ship got the job. It was a common practice in those days.

A 1954 Pennant School class picture with members of the Gray, Henneberry, Marryatt and Tough families represented. (MSHS) (Courtesy of Annie Gray of West Pennant)

In 1794, a small group of Loyalist settlers from Barrington, Shelburne County settled near East Pennant at Coote Cove, located at the western edge of Crystal Crescent Beach. By 1818, sixty-eight families were residing in the settlement. Over the next 150 years, families moved away and today all that remains of the Coote Cove settlement are the ruins of the stone cellars of the pioneers' homes.

Sambro

Sambro Harbour has been a haven for fishermen for centuries. Here, sailors from Europe who were fishing along the coast of Nova Scotia would go ashore to dry and salt their catch and replenish their fresh water supply. The Mi'kmaq called the community "Mesebakum" or "Mesebakunuk," which rather enigmatically means "the constant mocker." French fishermen referred to it as "Cesambre," which was anglicized to Sambro. There is evidence to suggest that the English had arrived along the shores of the harbour and were trading with the Mi'kmaq as early as 1698.

Sambro is at the furthermost part of the southeastern entrance to Halifax Harbour. The village is located near the head of Sambro

Harbour at the end of Route #306. Governor Cornwallis saw the need to populate the area with British settlers to deter a French attack by sea. So by 1752, three years after the founding of Halifax, twenty-six families lived and worked on Sambro Island, engaged in a thriving fishing industry.

Buildings located on Sambro Island situated off the coast of Sambro Head. (NSARM)

A lighthouse was built on the island from 1758 to 1760. It stands sixty-two feet on the top of the rocky island and is said to be the oldest standing lighthouse in Nova Scotia. The lighthouse has a long and colourful history. The first keepers were Joseph Rous and Michael Pennell. Pennell and his son, Michael Jr., were from the New England States. When Michael Pennell drowned near a shoal named for him, his son took over as keeper. Later members of the Gilkie family were in charge. The last keepers were John Fairservice and his wife, who lived there with their children from the mid-1960s until the late 1980s. They were among the very last keepers in Nova Scotia and Mr. Fairservice often told the tale of Big Alex, a soldier who either did himself in or was murdered by his compatriots for stealing the soldiers' pay. On dark nights when the keeper came down the steps after checking the light, he often heard footsteps behind him. Today the lens from the Sambro light is on display at the Maritime Museum of the Atlantic on Halifax's waterfront.

A cairn erected in honor of the Sambro Island Lighthouse, built in 1758 said to be the oldest lighthouse in Nova Scotia today. (NSARM)

A number of fishermen began settling on

the mainland, across from Sambro Island, including a group from Barrington Passage. According to folklore, they married local girls from Terence Bay since it was easier to sail to the bay to find a wife than manage the trek to Halifax. Among the very earliest settlers was a family by the name of Gray, who came from either Holland or Germany around 1779, and Elkanah Smith who arrived via Sherose Island in Shelburne around 1797.

Mr. William Gilkie of Sambro Cove ca.1950 sitting on a chair with a child on his knee and his wife and a friend, Edward Gallagher standing in the back. (NSARM)

Others from the Shelburne/Barrington area continued to settle in Sambro. American-born Caleb Nickerson, his wife, and nine children who were living in Barrington, along with Benjamin Barss Jr., a native of Barrington, all arrived in the Sambro area at the turn of the nineteenth century. Other family names of early settlers included the Gilkie, Flemming, Neal, Quinn, Ring, Saddler, Wilson, and Williams' families.

Near Sambro are three beaches within the Crystal Crescent Beach Provincial Park, of which one is crescent shaped. There is a marked ten-kilometer hiking trail that leads to the Pennant Point and the ruins at Coote Cove.

Bald Rock

Bald Rock is aptly named—it is dominated by a stretch of barren rocky coastline. The first land grants here were issued in 1772 to John Burbridge and William Best, and among the residents by the early mid-1800s were the families of James and Charles Gray, William and John Smith, and Richard Finley. Bald Rock no longer exists as a distinct community but has blended into nearby villages.

KETCH HARBOUR

The Mi'kmaq named the area around Ketch Harbour, "Nemagakunuk," meaning "a good fishing place." Some think the name Ketch Harbour may be a derivation of the Mi'kmaq word—a good place to make a "catch" of fish. In any event, the community, located about twenty kilometers from Halifax along Route #349, has been an important fishing spot for well over two hundred years. It is situated close to

Pilot boats from Atlantic Pilotage Ltd., in Halifax Harbour, transport pilots out to the entrance of the harbour to navigate for incoming ships. 1999 (AW)

the City of Halifax at a time when most travelled by boat. A fisherman's catch could be easily transported to Halifax by water for sale in the city's markets. That made it one of the earliest spots to be settled following the colonization of Halifax 1749.

By 1752, twenty-five people lived in Ketch Harbour. Within ten years it was known as Catch Harbour and a number of families had been issued grants, including those with the surnames of Brown, Richardson, Martin, and White. Thirty years later, by 1792, several more families had arrived, many of whom have descendants still living in the area. They included the Chapman, Flinn, Power, Mullins, Sullivan, Russell, Smith, Hackett, McCarthy, and Jones families.

Ketch Harbour, like Sambro, is known for its harbour pilots. In 1864, at the height of the American Civil War, Jock Fleming, born and raised in the area, defied a northern warship blockade of Halifax Harbour and sailed the Confederate States cruiser the *Tallahassee* out of the harbour by way of the narrow Eastern Passage.

Francis Mackie (MacKey), also of Ketch Harbour, was less fortunate. It was he who was the pilot on board the *Mont Blanc* on the fateful morning of December 6, 1917. The collision between the *Mont Blanc* and the munitions' ship *Imo* resulted in a catastrophic explosion that levelled most of the north and west ends of Halifax and Dartmouth, killed nearly two thousand and injured a further ten thousand. Mackie was charged for being at fault. He was eventually found not guilty, had his pilot's license returned, and spent many of his remaining years guiding ships in and out of the harbour.

The former family homestead of Francis Mackie (MacKey) in Ketch Harbour who was the pilot wrongfully charged with being responsible for the Halifax Explosion in 1917. (MSHS)

It has been a long time since pilots rushed down to the shore, hopped in to their rowboats, and raced each other to be the first to reach a ship requesting a pilot. Nowadays, tankers, cruise and cargo ships approaching the entrance to Halifax Harbour radio ahead and are met by a pilot who boards their ship off the coast of Chebucto Head, just above Duncan's Cove, and guides it through Halifax's harbour.

Duncan's Cove

Duncan's Cove, just over nineteen kilometers south east of Halifax, has a military history. One of the earliest families to settle in the area was Simon Duntoyn who arrived in 1752.

A scenic view of Duncan Cove showing the fish houses and sheds. (NSARM))

A photograph of John Holland taken ca. 1939 on his doorstep in Duncan Cove. (NSARM)

The headland above the cove overlooks the entrance to Halifax Harbour, a position that made it a strategic part of Halifax's defense system at the end of the eighteenth century. To facilitate the relaying of messages between outposts in the event of an attack on the town of Halifax, Prince Edward, Duke of Kent, erected the Camperdown Signal Station in 1797—one of the first such military signal stations in the province—and named the cove in honour of Admiral Duncan who had defeated the Dutch. The station was operational until 1925 when it was replaced by a more modern facility.

Over the years, a number of families settled around the cove, including those with the surnames of Crab, Full, Leonard, and John McNab who received fifty acres in 1859.

PORTUGUESE COVE

Portuguese Cove is thought to have received its name from the Portuguese fisherman who for many years sailed to the area in the summer months to fish. After salting and drying their catch at the cove, they would return home to Portugal. However, a number of local residents believe that the name refers to a Portuguese ship that was wrecked on the rocks nearby.

This area, located on Route #349, was once part of a large grant issued to Samuel Purcell in 1770 and to John Wild in 1786. In 1792, Peter, James, and John Martin (Marinis), fishermen from Genoa, Italy, arrived. Others came from Ireland, including Michael Fitzgerald who arrived in Nova Scotia with a number of his compatriots, all of whom had originally settled in Newfoundland. He first went to Ketch Harbour, finally moving to Portuguese Cove in 1810 with his wife and twelve children. John Thomas of South Carolina arrived in 1818 from Cape Cod, Massachusetts. Henry Bateman who had been living in the cove for a while received his land grant in 1821.

Doreymen, wharves and fishing sheds situated on Portuguese Cove ca. 1905. (NSARM)

Like many of the other small communities along this shoreline, some of the men were harbour pilots. By 1829, John Martin, John (Red) Fitzgerald, William Certile, George Sadler, Edward Bowers, and John Quan had all received their certificates. A descendant of the Fitzgerald's family became a hero on the Canadian frontier. Francis J. Fitzgerald died on February 7, 1911, in line of duty as a Royal Mounted Police inspector.

There is a bronze plaque dedicated to his memory placed in his honour on a footbridge in Halifax's Public Gardens.

Oral tradition maintains that the area around Portuguese Cove is riddled with hidden caves and tunnels. However, the children of the community have never discovered any of these sites while playing around the rocky coastline.

Herring Cove

Southwest of Halifax Harbour is a community that the Mi'kmaq called "Moolipchugechk" meaning "a deep chasm or gorge." Its present name, Herring Cove, more likely came from the abundance of herring often found in the cove. Some believe, though, that Tom Herring and his brother John settled here sometime around 1792 and may have given the cove its name. It is even listed on one of Governor Charles Lawrence's surveyor's maps as "Dunk Cove," a reference to George Dunk, Earl of Halifax.

The residents have earned their living from the sea since the first families arrived in the early 1800s—those with the names of Sullivan, Reyno, Pelham, Dempsey, and Brown. While a grant may have been given to John Salusburg sometime earlier, it was the Lather family who

Like most villages along this coastline, Herring Cove sits atop a granite rockface. (NSARM)

petitioned for title to the land in 1821, suggesting that Salusburg never lived on his grant, not an uncommon practice.

A photograph of George Brown of Herring Cove (1839–1875) who was a champion oarsman, (ca. 1870). (NSARM)

Herring Cove has had its share of famous individuals, especially those known for their skill in rowing competitions. George Brown was a champion singles sculler and for five years in a row he won the $150 belt offered by the Halifax Yacht Club. He is buried in St. John's Cemetery where there is a plaque in recognition of his rowing accomplishments. Another young man, Harold Johnson, a member of the Royal Canadian Mounted Police, was a talented rower and boxer. In 1926 he was a member of a team that won the rowing championships. He was known to win titles in both the Middle- and Light-weight boxing classes within the same night, which was considered to be an unusual achievement for a boxer. Henry Pelham, a member of the 1932 Olympic rowing team, rowed for the Halifax Rowing Club and won numerous medals and trophies.

Another Herring Cove hero was young Joe Cracker. As a very young child he lost his parents after they drowned in Portuguese Cove and he became a ward of the community. He was 13 years old when the HMS *Tribune* ran into trouble just off the coast. It was Joe who urged

Students who attended the Catholic School in Herring Cove, ca. 1913. (MSHS, courtesy of Rose Dempsey of Herring Cove)

the community to come to the rescue of the ship's passengers and crew. At first the captain would not accept help, believing he could handle the situation. But when it became obvious that the ship was doomed, Joe jumped into a small rowboat and was the first to row through the rough waters to rescue two survivors. Unfortunately the captain had delayed too long as only twelve of the 250 passengers on board survived.

FERGUSON'S COVE

West of Halifax Harbour, off the Purcell's Cove Road on Route #253 lies the small community of Ferguson's Cove. Settled in 1788, it was first known as Falkland after Lady Falkland, wife of Lucius Bentinck Falkland, one of the Lieutenant Governors of Nova Scotia at the time. Its present name may refer to an early settler.

A view of the rear encasements of a section of York Redoubt's fortifications in 1873, now a National Historical Site. (NSARM)

Among the first families to arrive were the Embleys, Glazebrooks, and Lynches. William Glazebrook arrived from England in 1788. The Lynch family from Ireland settled in the area by 1803. And William Embley, an Irishman from Newfoundland, served in the Royal Navy and moved to Ferguson's Cove after being discharged in 1811.

By 1827 some twenty-seven families had settled near the cove, among them Andrew Henneberry, John Lynch, Michael Lynch, William Scoles, Benjamin Brown, Samuel Wooten, and William Beverley. Within twenty years they had been joined by the Smith, Purcell, Holland, Harrington, Sullivan, Gifford, Horn, and Terrance families. Many of the men, like their compatriots along the coast, made a living as harbour pilots.

There is an eerie ghost story associated with the ships that have been wrecked on the dangerous reef off Ferguson's Cove. One stormy evening Richard Power was walking home when he saw a man gathering stones. The man extended an arm towards him that looked to be covered in blood. Mr. Power fainted and was found sometime later by workmen on their way home. The left side of his body had been burned black and he was paralyzed.

Near Ferguson's Cove is York Redoubt, which was constructed between 1793 and 1795 as part of Halifax's elaborate defense system to protect the harbour from attack. The crescent-shaped fort was part of Prince Edward's signal station communications. York Redoubt was renovated and expanded between 1863 and 1877 so it could be put to use once again. The fort is considered the first radar station to have been constructed in the world. In 1960 the site was declared a National Historic Site. During that decade, the fort was restored and it re-opened to the public in 1969, becoming a popular tourist attraction.

Purcell's Cove

Named for Samuel Purcell, an early settler, this cove sits opposite the tip of Point Pleasant Park on the North West Arm, along what today is known as Purcell's Cove Road. Before the Purcell family arrived, it was known as Mackerel Cove. The Purcells lived in the area for a number of years, but did not buy any land until 1828.

The McCurdy family home under construction in 1929. Today the home is used by the Royal Nova Scotian Yacht Squadron situated on the North West Arm in Purcell's Cove. (MSHS) (Courtesy of A.H. Longard)

In 1853, a descendant, John Purcell, operated a ferry between the cove and Point Pleasant Park. For more than a century, the family used rowboats and sailboats to ferry passengers across the Arm. There is still evidence of piers on both

sides of the North West Arm. Granite and ironstone were cut from the quarries near Purcell's Cove and were used to construct military forts in Halifax as well as many of the buildings on the Dalhousie University campus.

A photograph taken in the 1940s of the Purcell family's ferry. The family established the service in 1853, ferrying people across the North West Arm to a site on the shore of Point Pleasant Park until 1971. (MSHS) (Courtesy of Eric Salmonson of Halifax)

A Notman photograph taken ca. 1892 of the Purcell's Cove fishing village with schooners anchored in the cove. (NSARM)

JOLLIMORE

Jollimore was a suburb of Halifax on the North West Arm, situated off Purcell's Cove Road. The place is named for the family who first settled here. The original Jollimores were from Terence Bay who wanted to be closer to the city. The family realized the benefits of a ferry service across the North West Arm and were issued a license to carry passengers on their ferry. It was not until 1902 that the area was officially called Jollimore Settlement. It became a part of the City of Halifax on January 1, 1969.

The community includes Sir Sanford Fleming Park, known colloquially as "The Dingle" after American immigrant Richard Dingle. Sir Sanford is recognized as the Father of Time for creating the world's time zones. He was also instrumental in designing Canada's first postage stamp and played a major role in the development of the Canadian Pacific Railway.

In 1896, he donated land in Jollimore for a community church. Later, in 1908, he had the stone edifice known as the Dingle Tower erected and donated it to the City of Halifax to commemorate 150 years of representative government in Nova Scotia. The dedication took place four years later in 1912.

Located in Fleming Park is the memorial Dingle Tower overlooking the North West Arm and erected in 1912 to commemorate 150 years of representative government in Nova Scotia. (NSARM)

Melville Island ca. 1888. Some of the buildings used to house prisoners during the various wars are still standing, (NSARM)

Spryfield

The community of Spryfield situated on the Herring Cove Road is about six-and-a-half kilometers from Halifax's Armdale Rotary. The area was first settled by Henry Lieblin in 1767, a Halifax baker who received five hundred acres and named his home "Lieblin Manor." Today Lieblin Park Subdivision is located where his home once stood.

A Notman photograph taken ca. 1905 of the huge stone which can be rocked with little leverage, located on land formerly owned by the Kidston Family in Spryfield, now situated near Rockingstone Road. (NSARM)

The name of the community comes from an association with Captain William Spry, who received five hundred acres in 1769 joining another piece of property that he had purchased earlier. By 1771, he had purchased more land and was operating a 1500-acre Spryfield Farm. By 1783, he sold his home which included one hundred cleared acres and returned to England.

The Spry property was purchased by George MacIntosh who had bought other small grants along the North West Arm as far as Harrietsfield. He began to sell off the land as small lots. Today there is a new subdivision in Spryfield named for George MacIntosh.

Robert Letson, a Loyalist from New York, purchased one of the lots. Originally, Letson operated a sedan chair service from a stand on Barrington Street in downtown Halifax. He married three times and had a total of seventeen children.

Around 1800, the Jollimore and Boutilier families, both originally from the St. Margaret's Bay area, bought some of Letson's land, and in 1822 Richard Dingle of the United States purchased land around Letson

Lake. Sometime later, Henry Twinning, a Halifax barrister, built a summer residence he called "Boscobel" on land he bought from George Jollimore. The residence is now a registered heritage property.

By 1827, sixty-seven families were residing in the community, including those by the name of Brunt, Connors, Findlay, Henneberry, Kidston, Moor, Norris, Sutherland, and Warner. The Kidston family home at 62 Rockingstone Road, built in 1825, is also a registered heritage property. In 1831 William Lawson Jr. leased a mill for five years and operated a number of successful businesses, including a nail factory and a brewery that he owned with his brother Robert. Unfortunately, both the factory and the brewery were destroyed in a fire in 1839. In the meantime, Henry and George Lawson built a gristmill in 1838. By the mid 1850s, William Yeadon had purchased land around Williams Lake and erected a home on the Herring Cove Road.

Spryfield remained a small self-contained community until after World War Two. It was amalgamated as part of the City of Halifax, along with a number of nearby suburbs on January 1, 1969. Today Spryfield continues to grow with a library, shopping malls and other business enterprises being introduced into the Spryfield area.

Kidston Family in front of the oldest house in Spryfield built ca. 1825 by William Kidston who purchased land from the Lieblin and Bower grants as well as from George MacIntosh's estate. (MSHS) (Courtesy of Elsie Morash of Halifax.)

BIBLIOGRAPHY

BOOKS

The Africville Genaology Society, *The Spirit of Africville.* Halifax: Formac Publishing Co. Ltd., 1992.

Abucar, Mohamed. *Struggle For Development – The Black Community of North and East Preston and Cherry Brook; Nova Scotia, 1784-1987.* Dartmouth: Black Cultural Centre, 1988.

Akins, Dr. T. B. *The History of Halifax City.* Collections of the Nova Scotia Historical Society. Vol. VIII, Halifax: Morning Herald Printing and Publishing Company, 1895.

Bates, Jennifer L. E. *Gold in Nova Scotia.* Halifax: Department of Mines and Energy, 1987.

Belmore, Dolly. *The History of Caribou Gold Mines.* Halifax: Published by Author, 1990.

Bird, Will R. *This is Nova Scotia.* Toronto: McGraw – Hill Ryerson Ltd., 1972.

Blakeley, Phyllis R. *Glimpses of Halifax.* Belleville: Mika Publishing, 1973.

Brown, Joe . *The View From Here – An Oral History of Eastern Passage, 1864-1945.* Dartmouth: Shearwater Development Corporation, 1998.

Campbell-Kuhn, Margaret. *A Tale of Two Dykes.* Hantsport: Lancelot Press, 1982.

Chapman, Harry. *100 Candles – Dartmouth Natal Day, 1895-1995.* Dartmouth: The Dartmouth Historical Association, 1995.

Coady, Howard. *Sheet Harbour History – From the Notes of an Old Woodsman.* Hantsport: Lancelot Press, 1989.

Evans, Dorothy Bezanson. *Hammonds Plains – The First Two Hundred Years.* Halifax: Published by Author, 1993.

Fergusson, Bruce and Pope, William. *Glimpses into Nova Scotia History.* Hantsport: Lancelot Press, 1974.

Gilroy, Marion. *Loyalists and Land Settlement in Nova Scotia.* Halifax: Genealogical Committee and Royal Nova Scotia Historical Society, 1980.

Gray, M. Noreen and Smith, Annie S. Blois. *History Along the Old Guysborough Road.* Enfield: Published by Authors, 1987.

Hamilton, William B. *The Nova Scotia Traveller.* Toronto: MacMillan of Canada, 1981.

Hartlen, John. *Nova Scotia's Four Great Gold Rushes.* Halifax: Collections of the Royal Nova Scotia Historical Society, 1982.

Hartling, Phillip L. *Where Broad Atlantic Surges Roll.* Antigonish: Formac Publishing Co. Ltd., 1979.

Lakes, Salt Marshes and The Narrow Green Strip – Some Historical Buildings in Dartmouth, Halifax County and Eastern Shore. Halifax: Heritage Trust of Nova Scotia, 1979.

MacKinley, A. & W. *Description Sketches of Nova Scotia in Prose and Verse.* Halifax: Published by Author, 1864.

Martin, John Patrick. *The Story of Dartmouth.* Dartmouth: Published by Author, 1981.

Miller, Thomas. *Historical and Genealogical Record of the First Settlers of Colchester County.* Belleville: Mika Publishing Company, 1983.

Pachai, Bridglai . "Peoples of the Maritimes – Blacks." Halifax: Nimbus Publishing Ltd., 1997.

Pitcairn, Rev. Andrew. *A History of St. James Church and Jeddore – Commemorating 130th Anniversary.* Jeddore: Published by St. James Congregation, Rev. Andrew Pitcairn, Rector of Musquodoboit Harbour Parish, 1960.

Punch, Terry. *Inhabitants of Ship Harbour, Halifax County, 1820.* Halifax: The Nova Scotia Genealogist, 1991.

Raddall, Thomas H. *Halifax Warden of the North.* Toronto: McClelland and Stewart Ltd., 1977.

Regan, John. *Sketches and Traditions of the Northwest Arm, Halifax, NS.* Willowdale: Hounslow Press, 1978.

Sherwood, Roland. A*tlantic Harbours – People, Places and Events.* Hantsport: Lancelot Press, 1972.

Soucoup, Dan. *Maritime Firsts: Historic Events, Inventions and Achievements.* Lawrencetown Beach, Porter's Lake: Pottersfield Press, 1996.

Stephens, David. *It Happened at Moose River.* Windsor: Lancelot Press, 1974.

Tolson, Elsie Churchill. *The Captain, The Colonel and Me.* Sackville: The Tribune Press Ltd., 1979.

Walker, James W. St. G. *The Black Identity in Nova Scotia – Community and Institutions in Historical Perspective.* Dartmouth: Black Cultural Centre, 1985.

Watts, Heather. *Beyond the North West Arm: A Local History of William's Lake.* Halifax: William's Lake Conservation Co., 1979.

Withrow, Alfreda. *St. Margaret's Bay An Historical Album: Peggy's Cove- Hubbards.* Halifax: Nimbus Publishing Ltd. and Tantallon: Four East Publication, 1997.

Withrow, Alfreda. *St. Margaret's Bay-A History.* Tantallon: Four East Publication, 1985.

Wright, Esther Clark. *Planters and Pioneers of Nova Scotia.* Wolfville: By Author, 1982.

Newspapers and Periodicals

"Nova Scotia – Open to the World – Natural Assets." Halifax: *Atlantic Progress*, 1998
Eastern Shore Echo – March 31, 1977.
Halifax Chronicle – November 19, 1963.
Halifax Mail Star – August 29, 1964.
Liverpool Advance – February 12, 1913.
Mail Star – June 3, 1981.
Morning Chronicle – December 2, 1907.
Novascotian – April 21, 1856.

Brochures

Icelandic Memorial Society of Nova Scotia
Musquodoboit Trailways Association

Sources from the Nova Scotia Archives and Records Management

CS81 H173 G778 – "Haulin In the Net" by Linda Gray-LeBlanc (Includes a number of Communities around the Sambro/ Purcell Cove area) 1993.
F100 M94 Vol. 11 p. 210 – Chezzetcook
F107 B39 M91 Vol. 8 p.12-31 – R. V. Harris- History of Bedford and surrounding communities
F107 D25 L44 p. 247-58 – History of Dartmouth by M. Lawson (Includes other communities)
F107 P33 L75 – Peggy's Cove
F107 Sh3 R93 – Sheet Harbour
F120 Acl 1908 Vol. 8 p.26 – Prince's Lodge
F120 N42 .p #13 p. 84 – Prospect
F136 ON8r RO4 – 1904 p. 156-59 – Ship Harbour
F5018 C682 p. 415 1832 – Hammond's Plains
F5205 H251 L793 - Prospect
F5248 J54 F721 – History and Folklore – Includes a number of communities
F5248 J54 R167 – Jeddore, Owl's Head Harbour, Ship Harbour
F5248 S557 – Ship Harbour
F5249 C689 C189 – Cole Harbour
F5249 D975 R313 – Dutch Settlement

F5249 H173 B617 – History of Birch Cove
F5249 L424 D317 - Lawrencetown
F5249 M82 B878 – 1936 – Moose River Mine Disaster
F5249 M899 L913 – Moser's River
F5249 S557 - Ship Harbour
F80 C16re – Icelandic Settlers
F90 D15 Vol. 27 p.133, 1947 – Portuguese Cove
F90 N85 AR2P #7 – Halifax and surrounding areas
F90 N85 Ar2p #8 – Place Names of Nova Scotia by C. B. Ferguson
F90 N85 Vol. 22 – Halifax and surrounding communities
F90 N85 Vol. 22 – Halifax and surrounding communities.
F90 N85 Vol. 24 p. 88, 102-4 – Fletcher's Lake/Wellington
F90 N85 Vol. 24 p.176-90 – Oakfield, Wellington
F90 N85 Vol. 30 p.121 – Pleasant Point
F91 B81 1830 – Place Names by T. Brown (1922)
F92 D42M p. 9 – Oakfield and Wellington
J104 H6 Cap.97 1937 – Name change of Ship Harbour Lake to Lower Lakeville.
J104 H64 Vol. 12 1989 - An index of Communities within Nova Scotia that had their names changed by an Act of Legislature.
J104K3R29 1969 – Annex communities of Halifax and surrounding areas
LHM97 #55 1950-51 – Meagher's Grant
MG 1 Vol. 1468 #62 – Prince's Lodge
MG 1 Vol. 1767 #41 – Preston
MG 1 Vol. 1912 #1 – Sheet Harbour
MG 1 Vol. 2112 #10-14 – Cole Harbour
MG 1 Vol. 2433 #55 – Chaswood
MG 1 Vol. 2433 #55 – Musquodoboit Harbour
MG 1 Vol. 2856 #12 & 17 – Caribou Gold Mines, European Settlement Patterns
MG 1 Vol. 2864 – Notes on130 families of Eastern Shore Communities by R. K. Stevens
MG 1 Vol. 3034 # 8 – North West Arm
MG 1 Vol. 3034 #4 (1746-1906) – Birch Cove
MG 1 Vol. 3034 #5 - St. Margaret's Bay
MG 1 Vol. 3035 #2 - Sackville
MG 1 Vol. 3035 #6 - Middle Musquodoboit
MG 1 Vol. 733A #47 – McNab's Island
MG 100 Vol . 216 #19-44 – Various HRM Communities
MG 100 Vol. 109 #28 & 37 - Beaverbank
MG 100 Vol. 120 #45 – Lower East Chezzetcook
MG 100 Vol. 131 #15 – Lawrencetown

MG 100 Vol. 136 #33 – Duncan's Cove
MG 100 Vol. 14 # 109 – Jeddore
MG 100 Vol. 145 #25 – George's Island
MG 100 Vol. 166 #3 – Tantallon
MG 100 Vol. 166 #6 - Hubley
MG 100 Vol. 167 #17 – Indian Harbour
MG 100 Vol. 169 #16 - Jeddore
MG 100 Vol. 171 #24 – Kent Island (Pleasant Point)
MG 100 Vol. 171 #24 – Pleasant Point
MG 100 Vol. 171 #34 - Antrium
MG 100 Vol. 179 #9 – Lower Sackville
MG 100 Vol. 184 #32-33 – McNab's Island
MG 100 Vol. 186 #13 – Maroon Hall
MG 100 Vol. 194 #24 – Mushaboom
MG 100 Vol. 194 #38C & 39 – Musquodoboit Harbour
MG 100 Vol. 194 #42 – Elderbank
MG 100 Vol. 203 #48 – Oakfield
MG 100 Vol. 214 #12 – Cobequid Road
MG 100 Vol. 221 #3 – Jeddore
MG 100 Vol. 221 #3 – Ship Harbour
MG 100 Vol. 236 #14 – Tangier
MG 100 Vol. 237 #8 – Terence Bay
MG 100 Vol. 238 #15 – Three Fathom Harbour
MG 100 Vol. 244 # 25 - Wellington
MG 100 Vol. 244 #13 – Waverley
MG 100 Vol. 247 #33 – Windsor Junction
MG 100 Vol. 41 #77-78 – Moose River
MG 100 Vol. 42 #36 – Fort Sackville
MG 100 Vol. 43 p. 390 – Dover
MG 100 Vol. 49 # 44 – Salmon River
MG 100 Vol. 49 #44 – Port Dufferin
MG 100 Vol. 50 #140 – Lower Prospect
MG 100 Vol. 53 #86 – Harrigan Cove
MG 100 Vol. 57 # 66-64 – Porter's Lake
MG 100 Vol. 57 #22 – Conrod Settlement
MG 100 Vol. 58 #61 – Caribou Gold Mines
MG 100 Vol. 673 #3 – Cow Bay
MG 100 Vol. 72 #8 - Carroll's Corner
MG 100 Vol. 92 #22 – Little Harbour
MG 20 Vol. 673 #3 – Lawlor's Island and Easter Passage

MG 20 Vol. 677 #8 – Hubbards
MG 4 Vol. 115 p.3 – Mooseland and a number of Eastern Shore Communities.
MG 4 Vol. 247 #8-8A – Working Notes for "Place Names and Places of Nova Scotia"
MG 9 Vol. 188 p. 11 - Sackville
MG 9 Vol. 41 p. 119 – Musquodoboit Harbour
MG 9 Vol. 41 p. 162 – Sheet Harbour
MG 9 Vol. 42 p. 103 – Glen Margaret
MG 9 Vol. 42 p. 203 - Timberlea
MG 9 Vol. 42 p. 268 – Sheet Harbour
MG 9 Vol. 43 p. 344 - Birch Cove
MG 9 Vol. 43 p.390 - Dover
MG 9 Vol. 44 p. 102 – Owl's Head Harbour
MG 9 Vol. 44 p. 193 - Oakfield
MG 9 Vol. 45 p. 107 – Musquodoboit Harbour
MG 9 Vol. 45 p. 84 & 102 & 104 – Eastern Shore
MG 9 Vol. 46 p. 202 - Tantallon
O/S V/F Vol. 17 #7 – Chezzetcook Historical Society
V/F Vol. 117 #8 p. 8 – Dartmouth and surrounding communities
V/F Vol. 207 #7 - Waverley
V/F Vol. 273 #16 - Kinsac
V/F Vol. 280 #3 & # 1– Cherry Brook and Preston communities
V/F Vol. 328 #3 & #4 – Lewis Lake and Shad Bay
V/F Vol. 53 #30 – Herring Cove and surrounding communities
V/F Vol. 53 #30 – Pennant and Sambro area
V/F Vol. 54 #15 – Cherry Brook
V/F Vol. 64 #8 – Terence Bay
V/F Vol. 94 #10- Herring Cove and Sambro area.

Index of Community Names